License to Cook
New Mexico Style

This book introduces the spicy cooking of the Southwest with traditional dishes, fast and easy recipes, and new creations using traditional ingredients. Plus some highlights of "The L̲a̲

Collected by members of the New M̲
fessional Women from these chapters
City (Santa Fe), Duke City (Albuquer
Alamos, Lovington, San Juan (Farmington),
Tatum.

MW00987271

Editors: Esther Feske, Bobbie Rivera, Jane Viemeister, Joan Liffring-Zug, Miriam Canter, and Michelle Nagle Spencer. Thanks also for the assistance of Jane Garret, Joan Peterson, Michael Kaczor, Ross Edwards, Melody Viemeister, Georgia Heald, Dorothy Crum, and Kathryn Chadima. Cover and illustrations by Esther Feske.

BOOKS BY MAIL Stocking Stuffers POSTPAID You may mix titles. One book for $6.95; two for $12; three for $18; four for $22; twelve for $60. Each additional book: $5.

Please send $2.00 for complete price list. *(Prices subject to change.)*

Cherished Czech Recipes
Dandy Dutch Recipes
Dear Danish Recipes
Fine Finnish Foods
Great German Recipes
Intriguing Italian Recipes
Norwegian Recipes
Pleasing Polish Recipes
Recipes from Ireland
Scandinavian Holiday Recipes
Scandinavian Smorgasbord Recipes
Scandinavian Sweet Treats
Splendid Swedish Recipes
Waffles, Flapjacks, Pancakes, Crêpes,
    Blintzes, and Frybread from
    Scandinavia and Around the World

Breads
Buffets and Potlucks
Desserts
Fantastic Oatmeal Recipes
A Taste for Health (Low-Fat, Low-Cholesterol)
License to Cook Kansas Style
License to Cook New Mexico Style
Marvelous Minnesota Recipes
Outstanding Oregon Recipes
Recipes from the Hawkeye State (Iowa)
Southern Country Cooking
Wonderful Wisconsin Recipes
My Book (blank book, rosemaling design cover)

ISBN 0-941016-58-7
Copyright Penfield Press

PENFIELD PRESS
215 BROWN STREET
IOWA CITY, IA 52245-5842

Contents

Piñon nuts in and out of shell

So, Where's New Mexico?

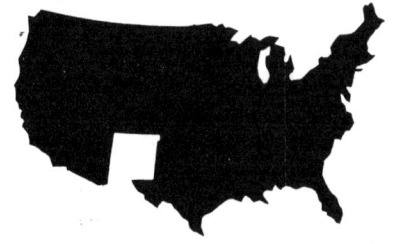

Is something missing? It's the only state that many Americans think is a foreign country. And it does seem that way sometimes, but you don't need a passport to visit, you don't need shots, and you can drink the water. Yes, New Mexico was once part of Mexico, but the United States claimed it in 1846. It's now part of the Sun Belt. Despite its many attractions, New Mexico still has a relatively small population, about one and a half million. Over one-third live in the middle of the state in the largest city, Albuquerque.

New Mexico includes the Native Americans who have been on the land for thousands of years. Many residents in the northern part of the state and in the capital, Santa Fe, can trace their ancestry directly to Spanish noblemen and explorers who came in the 1500s. Mexicans arrived somewhat later. "Anglos" and black Americans came to trade and settle after the Civil War. Most recently, Asian and Indochinese immigrants have found New Mexico a comfortable place.

The weather is ideal, high and dry mostly, but you can pick the climate you'd like, winter or summer, by altitude. If you're a Midwesterner, used to everything being various shades of green, you may be shocked to see lots of "bare ground." If you're an Easterner, used to humidity, haze and leaden skies, the great distances you can see in our dry air and open spaces may give you agoraphobia. If you're a Californian, used to crowded freeways and millions of people, you might enjoy the elbow room. (If you crave seeing lots of cars, drive Albuquerque's two freeways during rush hours.) And if the altitude gives you a headache or fatigue in the afternoon, two aspirin and a siesta work quite well for lots of people.

The Land of Enchantment

New Mexico is geologically complex: it's located where the Great Plains, Rocky Mountains, and range and basin landforms meet. It includes hot springs and artesian wells, caves, extinct volcanoes, old and recent lava flows, ash deposits, ancient coast and sea beds, upheavals and faults, the fifth largest river in the United States, and the Continental Divide. Elevations range from 2,800 to more than 13,000 feet above sea level and include six of the seven life zones found on earth, from Lower Sonoran to Arctic-Alpine.

Ten million acres are national forest land; another 13 million acres of public land are managed by the Bureau of Land Management. Native American pueblos and reservations occupy a smaller, yet significant portion of New Mexico. More than 44.6 million acres are in farms and ranches. There are some stretches of *malpais* (badlands) that are fun to visit but you couldn't live there.

Highlights of New Mexico

This is a brief list of popular things to see.

For further information, schedules of events, etc., write or call:

New Mexico Tourism and Travel Division
Joseph M. Montoya Building
1100 St. Francis Drive
Santa Fe, New Mexico 87503
In state: 505-827-0291 Out of state: 1-800-545-2040

For information on picnicking, camping, fishing, boating and other facilities in state parks, write or call:

New Mexico State Parks and Recreation Division
P.O. Box 1147, Santa Fe, New Mexico 87504
505-827-7465

Highlights of New Mexico

Alamogordo: Space Center, including International Space Hall of Fame; White Sands National Monument.

Albuquerque: Albuquerque Museum (art, history); Indian Pueblo Cultural Center; Museum of Atomic History; Museum of Natural History; Rio Grande Zoo; Old Town; Sandia Peak (accessible by car or the world's longest tram); "Turquoise Trail" (to Santa Fe through the mountains, ghost towns); Coronado National Monument (in Bernalillo); Petroglyph State Park.

Angel Fire, Red River, Eagle Nest, Cloudcroft, Sipapu: Camping, fishing, hiking, horseback riding, hunting, winter skiing, Rocky Mountain scenery.

Carlsbad: Carlsbad Caverns National Park.

Chama: Cumbres and Toltec Scenic Railway.

Chimayo: (On the "High Road" between Santa Fe and Taos) Famous for Spanish weaving.

Deming: Duck Races in August; City of Rocks State Park; Pancho Villa State Park; Rock Hound State Park.

Farmington Area: Salmon Ruins; Aztec Ruins National Monument; Chaco Culture National Historical Park; Four Corners (where Utah, Colorado, Arizona and New Mexico meet), numerous ruins and natural wonders.

Grants Area: El Morro National Monument (Inscription Rock); Bandera Crater/Ice Caves; El Malpais National Recreation Site.

Las Cruces: Organ Mountains; La Mesilla (original Spanish Plaza); Branigan Cultural Center; Fort Selden State Monument. From Las Cruces it's a short drive to El Paso, Texas, and Ciudad Juarez, Mexico.

Los Alamos Area: Bradbury Science Museum; Valle Grande volcano cone (in the Jemez Mountains); Bandelier National Monument and state parks: Indian ruins.

<u>Pueblos and Reservations</u>:

Each group has its own government, regulations and admission and camera fees. Cameras are prohibited at many events and at some pueblos entirely. Alcoholic beverages are generally prohibited. Various feast days are celebrated and open to the public; dates and times are not necessarily the same from year to year. You may call to find out about upcoming events.

1) **Isleta Pueblo** - 13 miles south of Albuquerque off I-25. Cameras are prohibited. 505-869-3111.
2) **Laguna Pueblo** - 45 miles west of Albuquerque off I-40. 505-552-6654.
3) **Acoma Pueblo** - Sky City - 40 miles west of Albuquerque off I-40. 505-552-6606.
4) **Zuni Pueblo**- 32 miles southeast of Gallup on NM 36 and 53. No cameras on ceremonial days. 505-782-4481.

5) **Sandia Pueblo** - 14 miles north of Albuquerque on I-25. No cameras, recording or sketching. 505-867-3317.

6) **Santa Ana Pueblo -** 8 miles northwest of the town of Bernalillo on N.M.44. No cameras, sketching or recording. 505-867-3301.

7) **San Felipe Pueblo** - 10 miles north of Bernalillo off I-25. No cameras, sketching or recording. 505-867-3381.

8) **Zia Pueblo** - 16 miles northwest of Bernalillo on N.M.44. No cameras, recording or sketching. 505-867-3304.

9) **Santo Domingo Pueblo** - Off I-25 between Albuquerque and Santa Fe. No cameras, recorders, sketching. 505-465-2214.

10) **Cochiti Pueblo** - West of I-25 about 45 miles north of Albuquerque. Cameras prohibited. 505-465-2244.

11) **Jémez Pueblo** - 50 miles from Albuquerque and northwest of Bernalillo off N.M.44. No cameras. 505-834-7359.

12) **Tesuque Pueblo** - Just north of Santa Fe. 505-983-2667.

13) **Pojoaque Pueblo** - 8 miles south of Española on U.S. 84. 505-455-2278.
14) **San Ildefonso Pueblo** - 25 miles northwest of Santa Fe on N.M. 502. Cameras prohibited on Easter. 505-455-2273.
15) **Nambé Pueblo** - 30 miles north of Santa Fe. 505-455-7692.
16) **Santa Clara Pueblo** - South of Española on N.M. 30. 505-753-7326.
17) **San Juan Pueblo** - 5 miles north of Española on U.S. 84. No cameras, recordings or sketching. 505-852-4400.
18) **Picuris Pueblo** - Off N.M. 68 between Española and Taos. 505-587-2519.
19) **Taos Pueblo** - 3 miles northeast of Taos. No cameras on ceremonial days. 505-758-9593.

20) **Navajo** - Part of the Navajo Nation is located in northwest New Mexico. Contact tribal offices in Window Rock, AZ, for regulations and fees. Northern Navajo Fair is in late September or early October each year at Shiprock, 30 miles west of Farmington on U.S. 84 and 666. 602-871-4941.

21) **Jicarilla Apache** - Dulce, the tribal capital, is at U.S. 84 and N.M. 537. 505-759-3242.

22) **Mescalero Apaches** - 18 miles northeast of Tularosa on U.S. 70. 505-671-4494.

<u>Raton</u>: Raton Pass on Interstate 25 from Colorado; Raton Museum; Capulin Mountain National Monument; (between Raton and Las Vegas): Santa Fe Trail remnants, Fort Union National Monument, Maxwell National Wildlife Refuge.

<u>Roswell</u>: Roswell Museum and Art Center; Spring River Park and Zoo; Bitter Lake National Wildlife Refuge.

13

<u>Santa Fe</u>:	The Museum of New Mexico, P.O. Box 2087, Santa Fe, New Mexico 87504, 505-827-6460: includes Museum of Fine Arts, Palace of the Governors (with Indians selling jewelry under its portal), Museum of International Folk Art, Museum of Indian Arts and Culture; Loretto Chapel; San Miguel Mission; Wheelwright Museum of the American Indian; historic Canyon Road; restaurants, shops and galleries; (nearby) Pecos National Monument; Rancho de las Golondrinas (restored Spanish ranch); Santa Fe Ski Basin; Santa Fe Opera.
<u>Silver City</u> :	Gila Cliff Dwellings National Monument; Santa Rita (one of the world's largest open pit copper mines); historic and mining sites.
<u>Socorro Area</u>:	Bosque del Apache National Wildlife Refuge (winter); Very Large Array (VLA) Telescope, world's most sensitive radio-telescope system.

14

Taos:	Ranchos de Taos (south of Taos); Kit Carson Home and Museum; Millicent Rogers Museum; Governor Bent Home and Museum; art galleries and shops; Taos Pueblo; Taos Ski Valley; Rio Grande Gorge Bridge.
Truth or Consequences:	Elephant Butte Reservoir and Caballo Reservoir on the Rio Grande.
Tucumcari:	Tucumcari Historical Museum; Conchas Lake State Park.

The zia (sun), symbol of New Mexico

The Peoples of New Mexico

10,000 B.C. Paleo-Indians, thought to be descendants of those who crossed the Bering Strait perhaps 30,000 years before, roamed the Southwest hunting bison. Language experts are currently studying the similarity between the Athapaskan languages (including Navajo and Apache) and some Asian dialects (Chinese and Mongolian).

6,500 to 6,000 B.C. The "Cody Period" was dominated by hunter-gatherers. Spearpoints found with the bones of extinct animals provide scientific evidence for dating.

600 to 800 A.D. Agriculture had been introduced from further south and four major cultures flourished in the Southwest: the Hohokam, who dug canals for irrigation for farming; the Anasazi, who built many multi-room buildings; the Mogollon, who lived in scattered farming settlements, and the Hakaytaya.

400 to 1300	Anasazi lived, prospered and eventually disappeared from what is now the Four Corners area of New Mexico, Arizona, Utah, and Colorado (including Mesa Verde in Colorado and Chaco Canyon in New Mexico). It is believed that prolonged drought forced them eastward to the Rio Grande Valley by 1300.
1050	The Mimbres people reached their high point, living in southern New Mexico. They are known for their beautifully detailed black and white pottery.
950 to 1100	Chaco Canyon, a major center of social and religious activity of the Anasazi, contains multi-storied buildings and roads radiating to outlying areas. Population is estimated to have been 5,000.
1535	Mesilla (near what is now Las Cruces) was a resting place for travelers; it later became a major crossroads on the Camino Real.
1536	The beginning of the Spanish exploration into the Southwest starting with Cabeza de Vaca. More than 100,000 native people of 40 tribes lived in the Southwest.

1540 to 1542	Don Francisco Vasquez de Coronado searched the Southwest for the fabled Seven Cities of Cibola. He visited many "pueblos" (Spanish for village or town). Unprepared for winter, he demanded food and hospitality.
1598	Don Juan de Oñate headquartered at San Juan Pueblo, establishing the first settlement and capital northwest of Santa Fe, nine years before the English arrived at Jamestown.
1610	Santa Fe was founded as capital of New Mexico.
1680	After years of oppression, religious pressure and exploitation, Pueblo Indians and Apaches pushed the Spanish out of Santa Fe, all the way to Juarez.
1692	Don Diego de Vargas recaptured Santa Fe and executed 70 Indian leaders, but Indian uprisings continued until 1696, the last revolt. Then the Spanish and the Pueblo Indians joined forces to subdue the nomadic and warlike Comanche who raided everyone. European diseases and strife had reduced native population by half.

1700 to 1800	Trade expansion and further exploration west continued. The Camino Real (Royal Road) was busy with caravans of traders between Santa Fe and Mexico City.
1706	Albuquerque, a small town with a church and farms along the Rio Grande, founded by Francisco Cuervo y Valdez.
1800	20,000 Spanish-speaking people of Spanish and mixed blood occupied the Southwest.
1807	American explorer Zebulon Pike and party were arrested as intruders; the governor wanted to prevent Anglo influences.
1821	Mexico declared independence from Spain and New Mexico became a province of Mexico. Santa Fe Trail opened with "Anglos" bringing trade between Santa Fe and Independence, Missouri.
1846	Mexican-American War began. General Kearny occupied Santa Fe, declaring it U.S. territory.
1848	Mexico formally ceded vast territories to U.S.

1850	Territory of New Mexico (now New Mexico and Arizona) established.
1853	Gadsden Purchase settled Mexico-U.S. border disputes.
Mid-1800s	Cattle and sheep ranching were major industries. Competition for grazing land often sparked violence and the land was overgrazed.
1862	New Mexico, originally declared Confederate in the Civil War, captured by the Union, preventing Confederate expansion to California's gold fields.
1864	8,000 Navajos were forced to march from northeast Arizona to Fort Sumner, New Mexico (580 miles) on the infamous Long Walk. Many died.
1870s	Cattlemen's War in Lincoln County attracted people like Billy the Kid. Arrival of Atchison, Topeka and Santa Fe Railroad (1879); by 1882 Southern Pacific also completed. Albuquerque doubled in size in this decade, as Santa Fe had been by-passed by the main line (Santa Fe got a spur in 1880).
1886	Raids by Apaches, the last to be subdued, ended with the surrender of Geronimo.
1912	New Mexico became the 47th state of the United States.

1930	Carlsbad Caverns became a national park.
1930s	Robert Goddard moved to Roswell to develop liquid-fuel rockets.
1943	Los Alamos Ranch School for Boys chosen to house the atomic energy project, and became a major nuclear research center.
1945	Trinity Site felt the world's first atomic bomb test, northwest of Alamogordo.
1950s	Postwar growth and air-conditioning allowed the Sun Belt to expand.
1957	Santa Fe Opera founded.
1970s	An economic boom in energy development, mining and oil, and solar energy research. New Mexico mines coal, uranium, copper, gas and oil, potash, gold, silver, lead, molybdenum, zinc and turquoise.
1990s	New Mexico's industries range from tourism, Native American crafts of weaving, pottery, and turquoise and silver jewelry to military installations, high-tech computer chip manufacturing, and "Star Wars" research. Agriculture produces cotton, sorghum, pecans, peanuts, beans, onions, lettuce, chiles, peaches, apples, wine grapes, corn, hay and grains. Santa Fe ranks third in the nation in art sales after Los Angeles and New York City.

Four Traditions

The Essence of New Mexican Cooking

New Mexican cooks have always made the best of what was available. From Pueblo Indians came corn, potatoes, beans, squash, wild game, sheep, domestic poultry, nuts, spices and a mild chile pepper they may have acquired in trade with neighbors to the south. Hot Aztec chile peppers, wheat flour, rice, garlic, citrus fruits, beef and pork were brought in by the Spanish Conquistadors (some from Spain and some picked up on their travels through the Caribbean and territory that would become Mexico). The opening of the Santa Fe Trail brought an influx of "Anglo" products as well as the Anglos themselves to the then-Mexican territory. This blending of Indian, Spanish, Mexican and Anglo cuisines is unique in New Mexico— not quite like Tex-Mex or Arizonan or Californian.

The Spanish language of New Mexico reflects this mix, as does the food, with words not only from Mexican, Anglo and Native American dialects, but also from the dialect spoken in 16th-century Spain which survived, little-changed for four centuries, in isolated mountain villages. Twentieth-century linguists have delighted in finding an antique form of a living language still being used.

Chile

Here the chile is king <u>and</u> queen. As mature green pods or ripe red dried pods, chile peppers in many variations of flavor and heat are pervasive. New Mexicans put green chiles on hamburgers, chicken sandwiches, pizza, in soup, stew or vegetables, or eat them alone. Red chile sauce is used on <u>anything</u>. The variations are literally endless—each cook, each restaurant, each commercial food processor has a favorite recipe, none quite alike. For instance, a red sauce might be mild and tomato-like or hot, raw and chunky with lots of onion, or cooked sauce so dark with mild chile that it's an earthy rich flavor, with only moderate heat. *(continued)*

We've included some red and green chile sauces if you'd like to make your own, or you can try every bottled sauce on the market until you decide which ones you like best. You're sure to enjoy the process of choosing.

Not enough can be said of chiles. New Mexicans—native or new—develop a craving for them. Their cars sport bumper stickers warning "Chile Addict." The most addicted may eat chiles every day. The newcomer may feel the need only once a week. Once addicted there is no cure. Late-summer visitors to New Mexico are begged to bring back fresh green chiles to former New Mexicans living in the Midwest. And in every New Mexican town, the smell of green chiles being roasted by street-corner vendors makes passers-by breathe deeply and salivate. Now, we could be analytical about how eating chile satisfies the mouth-hunger for stimulation, clears the sinuses, excites the digestion, soothes the stomach (to herbalists, chile is a carminative—stomach soother—in small doses!), and gives big quantities of vitamins A and C, but we who love them don't care. We just don't feel like we've EATEN until we've had our regular dose of chile. *(continued)*

24

Red chile is available as "ristras" (REE-strahs)—decorative bunches and strands of the drying red pods, or as ground powder, usually labeled mild, medium or hot. (See the Chile Heat Scale for the different varieties and their approximate "heat.") It is not the same as "chili powder" in a can, which includes other herbs. Red chile powder is simply the whole ripe red dried pods, ground up. Like other spices, it loses its punch in about a year, so if you want real chile flavor and heat, be sure it is fresh. You can even grind up your ristras in a blender, either dry or with a little water. To be authentic, red chile should be an important ingredient in commercially available "Taco Sauce," "Chile Sauce," "Picante Salsa" or whatever it's named.

If you hunger for the smell of green chiles roasting, you can roast and peel your own fresh green chiles. If not, perfectly acceptable green chiles are available canned, frozen, or dehydrated. They may be whole or chopped, mild, medium, or hot. Green and red chiles do not taste the same, partly because different varieties are usually used for the two colors. (Green chiles are harvested when full-sized, just before they turn red.) Green chile appears in dishes as chunks or whole, while red chiles are used ground or powdered. (continued)

By the way, you may encounter disagreement as to how to *spell* this vital vegetable (well, botanically, a fruit). A lot of New Mexicans will swear that chile is the plant and the fruit, while chili is that spicy meat and beans concoction. But, like a lot of other things in New Mexico, there are differences of opinion, stoutly defended. (For instance, every Christmas, most of the state refers to those brown paper bags with sand and candles in them which light the way of the Christ Child as "luminarias." Except Santa Feans, who insist they are "farolitos," and that "luminarias" are the bonfires that they intersperse with the bags.) The vast spaces and isolation of the past seem to have created an attitude that New Mexicans can pretty much do their own thing and should not interfere with someone else doing theirs. So, you'll likely get a variety of answers if you ask any question several times. Oh yes, chile might be pronounced "CHILL-ee" or "CHEE-lay" depending . . . .

Chile Heat Scale

Rating:	Chile Varieties:
10 Hottest	Bahamian, Habañero
9	Japanese Santaka, Chiltecpin, Thai
8	Piquin, Cayenne, Tabasco
7	de Arbol
6	Yellow Wax, Serrano
5	Jalapeño, Mirasol
4	Sandia, Cascabel, Rocotillo
3	Ancho, Pasilla
2	Rio Grande, Big Jim, Anaheim, NM-6
1	R-Naky, El Paso, Cherry,
0 No Heat	Bells, Pimiento, Sweet Banana

Chile Antidotes

So you made something with chiles and you sample it and it's too picante (pee-CON-tay) to eat? What to do?

—Add tomatoes (or tomato sauce or purée) for they soak up heat as well as spiciness.
—Serve with guacamole and/or sour cream; they're soothing and oily.
—Serve with or follow with something made with dairy products: cheese, ice cream, natillas, flan, even milk.
—Serve with or follow with citrus fruits or drinks or desserts (lemon pie, margaritas, sangria, daiquiris).
—Follow with something starchy: bread, potatoes, sopaipillas or fruit empanadas are perfect.
—Serve enough Mexican beer that your guests don't care how hot the chile is.

(continued)

Chile Antidotes   *(continued)*

If you're cautious, or you already know you want to make the dish less spicy next time:
—Use less chile; use milder chile.
—Do not use any canning liquid, it's just as hot as the chiles in it.
—Remove the seeds and membranes from chiles.
—Substitute bell peppers for all or part of the chile peppers.

Did you touch some chile or chile sauce that's burning your skin? The "heat" in chiles, capsaicin, is an oil, so washing with water won't work. Try washing with vegetable oil and soap to gradually dilute the capsaicin. And next time wear rubber gloves.

Tomatoes

Cousin of the chile peppers and green bell peppers, tomatoes blend so well with chile that some chile sauces have more tomatoes than chiles. The best sources of tomatoes are home grown and vine ripened from a farmer's market. Next best for flavor and consistency are canned tomatoes. Many cooks feel that the "fresh" tomatoes at the supermarkets lack flavor and have an unpleasant texture.

Beans

The next most important staple in New Mexican cuisine is Frijoles (free-HO-lays), beans: Pinto beans served in their own juices. Pink or pinto beans mashed and fried in lard until almost crispy. Beans and Spanish rice on every plate. Black bean and chile soup. Beans at every meal. If you do not want to go to the trouble of boiling beans, a good selection of canned beans is available in supermarkets, as well as several varieties of refried beans.

Tortillas

Right up there with beans is the tortilla (tor-TEE-yah) in its many forms: wheat flour tortillas served steamy with butter, flour tortillas wrapped around any number of fillings and steamed or fried; soft corn tortillas around fillings, corn tortillas fried into an envelope or cup to serve the main dish; tortilla wedges fried crispy and called taco chips, tortilla chips, or tostados (with an "o"). The Spanish conquistadors called loaves of bread *tortas*, so, when they saw the natives making their cornmeal and lime *masa* cakes, they called them the "little breads"—tortillas.

Flour tortillas vary from 6 to 10 inches across, regular or thick. They can also be torn into chunks and folded into little spoons to scoop up soup or sauce.

(continued)

Tortillas *(continued)*

Corn tortillas can be made of white, yellow or blue corn and are usually 6 inches in diameter. They differ in color, but only slightly in taste. Blue corn tortillas cook to blue-gray to black in color. Blue corn products (tortillas, pancake mix, corn meal) are available in New Mexico and are becoming available across the country.

Corn tortillas can be very hard and crispy or soft. They become hard and crisp when fried or baked dry. They are soft enough to cut with a fork when they are steamed or cooked with a liquid such as tomatoes or chile sauce. They can be softened if dipped in hot oil briefly, but not cooked, then drained on paper towels. To make taco shells from corn tortillas, fry briefly in hot oil, fold while still hot and soft and allow to cool and drain on paper towels.

(continued)

Tortillas   *(continued)*

Store corn and flour tortillas in the freezer if they won't be used in a week. Corn tortillas are wavy and separate easily when frozen. Flour tortillas may come already in food wrap, so they separate easily; otherwise, microwave the frozen package on high about one minute to thaw.

If you wish to make your own corn tortillas, look for "Masa Harina" at the supermarket. It is specially ground corn meal treated with lime (the mineral lime, not the citrus lime). Follow the instructions on the package. Masa Harina ("corn flour," pronounced MAH-sah are-EE-nah) is also used for tamales (masa, cooked shredded pork, and red chile rolled in a corn husk and steamed until well cooked).

If you wish to make your own flour tortillas, buy Masa Trigo (MAH-sah TREE-go) and follow the package directions. It is much easier to buy tortillas in a supermarket or deli. Similar flat breads are found in Middle Eastern and Chinese cultures.

33

To Fold a Flour Tortilla
for a Burrito or Chimichanga

1) Place filling in a strip down the middle.
2) Fold one side over filling.
3) Fold in the ends.
4) Continue rolling up, leaving the flap down so it holds itself shut for steaming or microwaving (for soft tortilla burritos), or frying (for crisp tortilla chimichangas).
5) Eat with a fork or pick it up and eat it like a hot dog.

*Folding
a burrito*

Posole

Posole is specially cooked and dried hard corn. Posole can be found canned, frozen or dried. Hominy is almost identical and can be substituted.

Piñon Nut

Piñon nuts are from a pine tree that grows in the Southwest. Trees must be very old before they make nuts, so piñon nuts are not grown commercially, but are gathered. Piñon nuts are expensive, but they have a unique taste.

Chorizo

Chorizo (cho-REE-zoh) is a spicy Mexican-Spanish-Portuguese sausage. To use chorizo remove it from the casing, crumble or slice and cook well.

Typical Flavorings

Anise seed, basil, canela (coarse stick cinnamon), cominos (whole or ground cumin), cilantro (fresh coriander or Chinese parsley), chile peppers, sweet bell peppers, garlic, lemon and lime, manzanilla (camomile flowers), onions, oregano, piloncillo (chunk brown sugar) and thyme.

Beverages

Vinos y amores, viejas son mejores.
Love and wine, the older the better.

Con vino y esperanza todo se alcanza.
With wine and hope everything is attainable.

Salud, dinero y amor y tiempo para gustarlos.
Health, money and love and time to enjoy them.
—*A Spanish toast*

Easy Margaritas

12 oz. Tavern's Sweet and Sour

6 oz. tequila
8 ice cubes, broken up

Put in blender jar and freeze for 24 hours. Then blend and serve as needed.

Variation: For a Margarita Gold, add 1 jigger Grand Marnier and 2 tablespoons of cream or half-and-half.

Cantaloupe Refresher

3 medium-sized cantaloupe   1/2 cup honey
1 1/2 cups cold water   12 large ice cubes

Seed and peel cantaloupe. Cut into small cubes and purée in blender. Add a little of the cold water as needed. Stir in honey after cantaloupe is completely puréed and dissolve. Add remaining water and ice cubes. Blend. Chill before serving.

Variation: Use 2 pounds of strawberries instead of cantaloupe plus the juice of one lemon. Place strawberries in blender and blend, adding water as needed. When blended, put through a fine sieve. Add lemon, honey, water and cubes and blend until smooth. Serve cold.

38

Sangría Punch

1/2 cup lemon juice
1/2 cup orange juice
1/2 cup sugar

1 quart of dry red wine
1/2 cup peach or apricot brandy
1 large bottle club soda, chilled

To do ahead: Freeze water in Bundt pan to make ice ring for punch bowl.
Just before serving: Pour juices and sugar into punch bowl; stir until sugar is dissolved. Stir in remaining ingredients. Unmold ice ring and gently slide into punch bowl. Makes 10 cups.

Variations: Using a mixture of orange and lemon juice and half water for your ice ring will make the last glasses of punch as tasty as the first. You may also float thin slices of lemon, orange and peach in the bowl and serve a piece of fruit in each cup.

Fresh Peach Daiquiri

4 medium-sized fresh peaches,
    peeled and chopped
2 Tbs. water

2 tsp. lemon juice
2 tsp. powdered sugar
2 oz. light rum
crushed ice (optional)

Purée peaches and water in blender until smooth. Blend in remaining ingredients and crushed ice, if desired. Serve in chilled glasses. Makes 2 servings.

Try this with nectarines and pears, too!

Frosty Fruit Punch

1 12-oz. can frozen orange juice
    concentrate
1 6-oz. can pineapple juice
    concentrate
1 6-oz. can lemonade
    concentrate

1 qt. pineapple sherbet
1 qt. lime sherbet
1 1/2 qts. ginger ale or lemon-lime
    carbonated beverage, chilled
fresh mint leaves

Prepare orange and pineapple juice according to directions. Prepare lemonade using only 3 cans of water. Combine and chill. At serving time, pour chilled juice mixture into punch bowl. Add sherbets scoop by scoop. Slowly add ginger ale. Garnish with fresh mint leaves. Makes 25 to 30 servings.
Good for Christmas or anytime.

41

Mexican Chocolate

1/4 cup sugar
2 Tbs. flour
1/4 cup cocoa
1 1/2 cups cold water
1/4 tsp. salt

1 tsp. cinnamon
3/4 tsp. cloves
6 cups milk
1 Tbs. vanilla
whipped cream
nutmeg

Combine sugar, flour, cocoa, water and spices in saucepan; cook about 4 minutes over medium heat. Add milk and scald, do not boil. Stir. Add vanilla. Serve with biscochitos (recipe found on page 149). Top each cup with whipped cream and a sprinkle of nutmeg.

Sauces and Dips

Pots from early pueblo ruin

Every calculation based on experience elsewhere fails in New Mexico.
—*Lew A. Wallace, territorial governor of New Mexico from 1878-1881, and author of Ben Hur.*

Salsa Fría Verde

(SAHL-sah FREE-a VAIR-day)
Uncooked Green Chile Sauce

4 tomatoes, peeled and finely chopped
1/2 cup minced onion
1/2 cup minced celery
1/4 cup minced green pepper
1/4 cup olive oil

3 Tbs. chopped mild green chiles
1 tsp. mustard seed
1 tsp. ground coriander
1 tsp. salt
dash pepper

Combine ingredients, cover and chill for several hours. Serve as a mild dip for tortilla chips or as a sauce for other dishes. Makes 6 cups.

Blue Ribbon Salsa

An authentic and basic green chile salsa.

4 tomatoes, chopped fine
2 bunches green onions, chopped fine
3/4 cup chopped green chiles or
      to taste

1 sprig fresh cilantro
1/4 tsp. salt
1/4 tsp. garlic powder
1 tsp. vegetable oil

Combine all ingredients and refrigerate several hours for flavors to blend well. Use on tacos and tostadas, in quesadillas, as a side to any meat dish, or, if you're brave, to dip tortilla chips into. The "heat" will vary, depending on the variety and quantity of chiles used.

45

Basic Red Sauce

This is the basic, all-purpose sauce for enchiladas, red chile and meat, tacos, and burritos. New Mexicans use the chiles from their ristras (a large string of red chiles) to make this sauce.

10 to 12 dried whole chiles
1 large onion, chopped

3 cloves garlic, chopped
3 cups water

Place the chiles on a baking pan in a 250° oven for about 15 minutes or until the chiles smell like they are toasted, being careful not to let them burn. Remove the stems and seeds and crumble into a saucepan. Add the remaining ingredients, bring to a boil, reduce heat and simmer for 20 to 30 minutes or until the chiles are soft. Purée the mixture in a blender and then strain. If the sauce is too thin, place it back on the stove and simmer until it is reduced to the desired consistency. Makes 2 to 2 1/2 cups. Freeze in small containers for future use.

Red Chile Sauce

A good basic sauce for every use.

1 clove garlic, minced
3 Tbs. olive oil or lard
2 Tbs. flour

1/2 cup ground red chile
2 cups water
salt to taste

Sauté garlic in oil. Blend in flour; add chile powder and blend. (Don't let pan get too hot as chile will burn.) Blend in water and cook to desired consistency. Add salt to taste. Store in refrigerator or freezer.

Red chile ristra

Salsa Jalapeña

(SAHL-sa hal-a-PAIN-ya)

This is wonderful, but you can't eat too much of it.

3 fresh tomatoes
5 fresh jalapeños

6 green onions
3 small leaves of cilantro

Dice tomatoes, jalapeños, onions and cilantro. Mix well together.
Goes very well on posole and tacos, or as a dip for warm corn tortillas.

Pico de Gallo
(PEE-co day GAH-yo)

This uncooked sauce (called "beak of the rooster!") is served with fajitas.

3 tomatoes
3 Spanish onions or red onions or both
3 small avocados

3 to 6 jalapeños, depending on
    how hot you like it
3 leaves fresh cilantro, chopped fine

Dice ingredients into 1/2-inch cubes and mix together. Refrigerate a few hours to let flavors blend.

Note: Dried cilantro does not work as well as fresh in this recipe. Fresh cilantro is found at grocery stores. Cilantro is fresh coriander, sometimes called Chinese parsley.

Hot Taco Dip

2 4-oz. cans mild green chiles
1 Tbs. vegetable oil
1 Tbs. red wine vinegar

2 bunches green onions, thinly sliced
1 28-oz. can tomatoes, well chopped
5 to 10 chile piquins

In a blender, mix the green chiles, oil and vinegar. Remove mixture from blender and add chile piquins, green onions and tomatoes. Use 5 chile piquins to make the dip medium hot; 10 for hot. Serve as a dip for tortilla chips or as a spicy-hot salsa with other dishes. Makes 5 1/2 cups. Chile piquins are small, very hot chile peppers.

Green chile

Chile con Queso Dip

2 Tbs. butter
1 Tbs. flour
1 cup milk
dash each of salt, pepper and
      garlic powder

1 cup grated Cheddar cheese
1 4 -oz. can diced green chiles
1 or 2 diced jalapeño peppers
    (if you like it hot)

Melt butter, blend in flour; add milk. Bring to a fast boil, stirring constantly. Add seasonings, cheese, chiles and peppers, if desired. Cook over medium heat until thickened. Makes 1 3/4 cups.

Note: A popular New Mexican short cut is to use Velveeta instead of Cheddar cheese and flour.

51

Chili Bean Dip

A spicy-hot dip—serve with corn chips!

1 16-oz. can chili hot beans
2 cups dairy sour cream

2 Tbs. minced onion
2 Tbs. minced green pepper
dash garlic powder

Mash beans with their liquid. Blend in remaining ingredients and heat through; do not boil. Serve warm. Makes about 4 cups.

Note: If chili hot beans are not available, use pinto beans and drain before mashing. Season with chili powder to taste.

Guacamole 1

1/4 small red onion, chopped finely
1 tomato, seeded and chopped
2 large (3 if smooth with large pit)
    avocados, peeled, pitted
    and mashed

1 or 2 garlic cloves, mashed
1 tsp. salad oil
3 Tbs. lime juice
salt and pepper to taste

Mash all ingredients in a bowl.   Or process onion and garlic in a food processor; remove. Add tomato (do not overprocess tomato or you will get juice); remove. Add avocado, oil, lime juice. Mix all together. Processing the vegetables this way allows you to control the texture better.

Guacamole 2

(gwa-cah-MO-lee)

4 ripe avocados
2 Tbs. fresh lemon juice
1 tomato, peeled and finely chopped
2 green onions, chopped

1 mild green chile, chopped
(or more to taste)
salt and pepper to taste
garlic powder to taste (optional)

Peel, pit and mash avocados. Add lemon juice, tomato, onions, green chile, salt, pepper and garlic powder. The dip may be served chunky or processed in the blender if a smoother texture is desired. To prevent the guacamole from turning dark, place the avocado pits on top of the dip, cover tightly with plastic wrap, and refrigerate until serving time, but not more than 4 hours. Makes 4 cups. Serve as a dip for chips or endive leaves or as a dressing on a lettuce salad.

Heavy-Duty Nacho Sauce

For nachos, you can always heat a jar of Cheez-Whiz in the microwave and pour it over corn chips. Or you could make this beer-cheese sauce. It is so good that you can dip tortilla chips or even steamed flour tortillas in it—and call it a meal!

1 cup chopped onion
2 medium-sized cloves garlic, crushed
1/4 cup olive oil
1/2 tsp. ground cumin
1/2 tsp. ground coriander
1/2 tsp. mild red chile powder,
      or more to taste
1 tsp. salt

1/4 tsp. freshly ground black pepper
1 bell pepper, chopped
2 tomatoes, chopped
1/4 cup flour
1 12-oz. can beer at room temperature
2 cups grated brick or Monterey
      Jack cheese

(continued)

Heavy-Duty Nacho Sauce   *(continued)*

Sauté onion and garlic in olive oil with spices and salt. When onion is translucent, add peppers and tomatoes; sauté 10 minutes more. Stir in the flour and cook 5 to 10 minutes. Add the beer and cook over medium heat another 15 minutes, stirring often. Cover and turn heat very low and let simmer an hour or two or three, stirring every 15 minutes. Uncover and remove from heat and let cool, about 45 minutes. To serve, reheat slowly, sprinkle in the cheese as it melts. Serve hot.

Appetizers

Trust everybody. . .but brand your calves.
—Randy Rubin, Raton merchant

The more you pay for an item, the more it's worth.
—Charles Dickerson, Las Cruces auctioneer

Ancient animal fetishes

Nacho Appetizer

Nachos with everything on them.

12 corn tortillas
oil for deep frying
1/2 lb. chorizo sausage
1/2 lb. lean ground beef
1 large onion, chopped
2 16-oz. cans refried beans

1 4-oz. can mild green chiles, chopped
12 oz. Monterey Jack cheese, grated
3/4 cup bottled taco sauce
1/4 cup chopped green onion
1 avocado, peeled, pitted and mashed
1 cup sour cream

Cut tortillas into wedges. Fry in hot oil until crisp. Drain on paper towels and salt to taste. Remove casing from sausage and crumble into skillet. Sauté sausage, ground beef and onion until meat is well cooked.

(continued)

Nacho Appetizer *(continued)*

Pour off grease and add salt to taste. On a 10x15-inch baking dish or large oven-proof platter, spread refried beans and top evenly with meat mixture. Cover with chiles. Sprinkle with grated cheese. Drizzle taco sauce over cheese. (This may be covered and refrigerated at this point for later use.) Bake uncovered at 400° for 20 to 25 minutes or until hot. Remove from oven, sprinkle with green onions. Put a mound of mashed avocado in the center, and put dollops of sour cream over all. Place fried tortilla pieces around edges of platter and serve. Keep appetizer warm over a warming tray. This may be served as an appetizer for about 12 people. It may also be a casual main dish for 4 to 6 people.

Party Taco Dip

1-lb. can refried beans
2 to 3 ripe avocados, peeled and pitted
garlic powder, to taste
lemon juice, to taste
1-lb. container sour cream
1/2 pkg. taco mix seasonings

1 to 1 1/2 cups shredded lettuce
1/2 cup chopped onion
1 cup chopped tomato
1 cup chopped green pepper
shredded Cheddar cheese, to taste
sliced ripe olives, to taste

Warm refried beans, then spread on a large serving platter. Mash avocado with garlic powder and lemon juice to taste. Spread over refried beans leaving the edges of the beans showing. Whisk together sour cream and taco seasonings. Spread over the avocado layer leaving the edges of the avocado showing. Continue to build with layers of lettuce, onion, tomato, green pepper, and Cheddar, leaving the edges of the previous layer showing. Top with olives and serve with tortilla chips and/or vegetables.

Empanadas
Little Pie Appetizers

1/2 lb. lean ground beef
1/4 cup minced onion
3 Tbs. red chile salsa, hot or mild
1 tsp. chili powder

1/2 tsp. ground cumin
1/2 tsp. garlic powder
1/2 tsp. ground coriander
salt and pepper to taste
10-oz. pkg. frozen patty shells, thawed

Crumble beef and sauté with onion in a skillet until beef is cooked and onion is soft. Drain. Stir in red chile salsa and spices. Set aside. Place thawed patty shell dough on a floured board and roll out, in one piece, to about 1/16 inch thickness. Cut dough into 3-inch rounds, about 20. Put 2 teaspoons of filling on each dough circle; fold in half. Moisten edges with water and press edges together with a fork. Place on ungreased cookie sheet. Prick tops with a fork. Bake at 400° for 20 minutes or until golden brown. Serve hot. (These may be wrapped after baking and frozen. To reheat, bake frozen uncovered at 400° for 7 to 8 minutes.)

Taco Chicken Wings

2 1/2 to 3 1/2 lbs. chicken wings,
    tips removed
1/2 cup buttermilk baking mix

1 1/4-oz. pkg. taco seasoning mix
1/3 cup butter or margarine
1 cup crushed corn chips

Rinse chicken wings and pat dry with paper towels. Cut in two at the joint. Combine baking mix and taco seasoning mix; dredge chicken to coat evenly. Melt butter in 10x15-inch baking pan. Place chicken wings in pan and turn to coat evenly with butter. Roll chicken in corn chips and return to pan. Bake uncovered in a preheated 350° oven 35 to 45 minutes. Makes about 24 to 34 pieces.

Spiral Appetizers

Tasty and popular at parties.

8 oz. cream cheese
1/2 cup chopped mild or
      medium green chiles

1 pkg. large flour tortillas
2 avocados, cubed (optional)

Mix together the cream cheese and chiles. Cut large tortillas in half, or use smaller ones whole. Spread the cream cheese mixture evenly over the tortillas, about the same thickness as the tortillas themselves. Roll up (from cut side if using large tortillas). Slice roll into 1/2-inch segments. Lay spiral flat on serving tray, or skewer a toothpick through an avocado cube and through the spiral.

Green Chile Cheese Ball

1 8-oz. pkg. cream cheese, softened
1/4 cup chopped green chiles,
     or more to taste

dash garlic powder
paprika
crackers or heavy corn chips

Thoroughly mix cream cheese, chiles and garlic powder. Form into a ball on the center of a piece of plastic wrap. Bring up sides of wrap and secure with a rubber band. (This will hold the shape of the ball.) Chill several hours. Remove from plastic wrap. Sprinkle with paprika to cover. Serve with crackers or corn chips.

Chorizo Cheese Tarts

12 taco shells or corn tortillas
    shaped like cups
2 egg yolks, beaten
1 12-oz. pkg. Mexican chorizo or hot
    Italian sausage
oil

1/4 cup minced onion
1 16-oz. jar or can chunky salsa
2 eggs, beaten
6 oz. Mexican Chihuahua cheese or
    Monterey Jack cheese, grated
1/4 tsp. oregano

Heat oven to 350°. Brush shells or cups with beaten egg yolks and bake for 3 minutes. Remove from oven. To prepare filling, remove the sausage from the casing and brown in oil. Add onions and sauté until the onions are soft and the sausage is well done. Mix salsa with beaten eggs. Spoon sausage mixture into tarts. Pour salsa-egg mixture over the sausage. Cover each tart with grated cheese. Dust with oregano. Bake at 350° for 20 to 25 minutes. Makes 12 servings. Serve as an appetizer or main course.

Chili, Stews & Soups

"You can keep your dear old Boston, home of beans and cod,
we've opted for New Mexico and chile, the fire of the Gods. . ."
—*Miles Standish IV, while visiting Kit Carson in Taos, New Mexico, 1842.*

To live well is the best revenge.

—*Old Spanish Proverb*

*Hot little
chile piquins*

Minute Chili

A quick-to-fix spicy-hot chili with surprise ingredients!

15-oz. can tamales in chili sauce
15-oz. can chili with beans
16-oz. can tomatoes, coarsely cut up

10-oz. pkg. frozen whole kernel corn
1/4 to 1/2 cup water
shredded Cheddar cheese

Remove tamales from their wrappers and cut into bite-sized pieces; gently stir into chili in medium-sized saucepan. Add remaining ingredients. Cover and simmer 10 to 15 minutes or until corn is tender. Garnish each serving with shredded Cheddar cheese. Makes about 6 cups.

Mountain Man Chili

1 lb. salt pork, cubed
4 lbs. coarsely ground meat (beef
    elk, venison, etc.)
3 7 1/2-oz. cans tomato juice
4 cubes beef bouillon
4 Tbs. ground cumin

4 to 6 cloves garlic, mashed
1/2 to 1 tsp. cayenne
3/4 cup mild chili powder (if hotter
    than mild, omit cayenne)
2 to 4 1-lb. cans dark red kidney beans
1 qt. water

Fry salt pork until crisp; discard salt pork and keep fat. Brown meat in fat. Add remaining ingredients. Cook overnight in a crock pot or 3 to 4 hours on a stove top.

Variation: Fry the meat in the ground cumin first.

Quick Vegetarian Chili

1 onion, chopped
oil
3 15-oz. cans beans, drained (choose
   pinto, pink kidney, red kidney,
   Northern and/or garbanzo beans)
2 or 3 1-lb. cans tomatoes

2 carrots, sliced
1/2 cup uncooked lentils
1 to 2 tsp. chile powder, to taste
1 Tbs. parsley
grated Cheddar cheese
tortilla chips

In a 3-quart or larger saucepan, sauté onion in a little oil. Add beans, tomatoes, carrots and lentils. Mix well. Add chile powder to taste (make it milder than you want; "heat" will accumulate as you eat the chili) and parsley. Simmer 1/2 hour, or until carrots are cooked. Serve in large bowls, topped with grated Cheddar cheese; serve with tortilla chips. 4 generous servings.

Corn Off the Cob Chowder

2 Tbs. butter
1 cup chopped onion
1/2 cup each, chopped red and
    green pepper
4 cups fresh sweet corn (4 to 5 ears)

1 cup chicken stock
1 cup evaporated milk
1/2 tsp. salt
1/2 tsp. basil
1/4 tsp. thyme
freshly ground pepper

In a medium-sized pot, cook onions in butter until clear, add peppers, corn and seasonings. Lower heat, cover and cook 5 minutes. Add stock and simmer 10 minutes. In a blender, purée half the solids in some of the liquid. Add back to the pot and mix well. Add milk and heat gently before serving. Serves 3 to 4.

Green Chile Stew

1 1/2 lbs. lean pork, round steak, or
    a mixture of both,
    cut into1/2-inch cubes
oil
1 medium-sized onion, chopped
4 cups water
4 medium-sized potatoes, cubed
3 large cloves garlic, minced
2 tsp. salt
1/3 tsp. pepper
1 lb. green chiles, chopped
2 medium-sized tomatoes, cubed

In large saucepan, brown meat in a little oil for 15 minutes over medium heat, stirring frequently. Be sure meat is well-browned. Add chopped onion, continuing to brown for 5 minutes. Add water and potatoes, and fast simmer for 15 minutes, or until potatoes are done. Add green chiles, tomatoes, garlic, salt and pepper. Simmer for 10 minutes, stirring frequently. Makes 2 quarts.

Sopa de Pescado

(SO-pa day pays-CAH-doe)
Fish Soup

1 lb. white fish, boned and cubed
1 pkg. frozen chopped spinach,
    thawed and squeezed dry
1 12-oz. can vegetable juice cocktail
4 chicken bouillon cubes

4 cups water
1 medium-sized onion,
    quartered and sliced
1/2 cup small salad pasta
1 small can chopped green chiles

In a 4-quart saucepan, combine spinach, vegetable juice cocktail, bouillon cubes, water, and sliced onion. Simmer until bouillon cubes are dissolved and onion is tender, about 15 minutes. Add the fish and the green chiles. Simmer until fish is opaque and cooked through (test a piece with a fork to see if it flakes easily). Meanwhile, in another pot, cook the pasta in boiling water until it is tender. To serve, divide the pasta among heated serving bowls. Ladle soup on top. Hot tortillas or corn bread muffins are a nice accompaniment. Serves 6.

Posole

(po-SO-lay)

Posole is the traditional Christmas Eve meal, eaten after viewing or participating in the neighborhood "Posadas"—a reenactment of Mary and Joseph going from door to door, looking for a place to stay.

1 pkg. dried or frozen posole
water
2 medium-sized onions

4 whole cloves garlic, crushed
2 lbs. lean pork, cubed
red chile, to taste

Cover the posole with water and bring to a boil. Pour the water off and continue this process until the boiled water is clear. Cook posole in water until corn pops, approximately 2 hours for dried and 30 to 45 minutes if using frozen. Add remaining ingredients and simmer slowly until meat is tender, approximately 2 hours. Add water as necessary to prevent scorching. Use either powdered or frozen chile.

Mexican Avocado Soup

1 medium-sized avocado
2 cups milk
1/4 cup sour cream
1/4 tsp. salt
1/2 tsp. cumin

fresh ground black pepper
cayenne pepper to taste
1/2 cup finely minced red onion
1/2 cup canned green chiles, minced
tortilla chips as garnish

Peel and pit the avocado and cut into small pieces. Put into blender or food processor and purée until quite smooth. Pour into a bowl. Add remaining ingredients and mix well. Cover the bowl and chill until cold. Garnish with tortilla chips on top of each serving. Serves 4.

Tacos, Burritos & Enchiladas

La mujer solo manda en la cocina, y en la esquina,
y en la plaza, y en el mundo.
The woman is the boss <u>only</u> in the kitchen—<u>and</u> on the corner,
<u>and</u> downtown, <u>and</u> the whole world.

Taco

Tacos

1 small onion, chopped
2 Tbs. oil
1 lb. ground beef
1 large tomato
2 medium-sized potatoes, cooked
    and diced
1/2 tsp. crushed oregano

1 tsp. comino (cumin powder)
12 taco shells
1 1/2 cups grated longhorn or
    Monterey Jack cheese
green chile salsa
shredded lettuce
sour cream (optional)

Sauté onions in oil, add meat and fry until well done. Add tomato, diced potatoes, and seasoning; blend well. Fill each taco shell with 2 tablespoons of mixture. Top with grated cheese and salsa. Place in baking dish and bake in a 400° oven for a few minutes for cheese to melt. Before serving, garnish with shredded lettuce. Serve with sour cream if desired.

Taquitos
(tah-KEE-tohs)
Rolled Tacos

2 dozen corn tortillas   shortening for frying

Use same filling as for tacos. Dip one tortilla at a time in hot fat to soften; drain. After all tortillas have been dipped, place 2 teaspoonfuls of taco filling in center, spread across width of tortilla, then roll. Secure with toothpick, fry in deep fat until crisp.

Note: Taquitos are good dipped in taco sauce, sour cream or guacamole.

 *Taquitos*

Flautas
(FLAOW-tus)

So named because they have the shapes of flutes.

1 lb. ground beef
2 cups chile sauce, divided

1 1/4-oz. pkg. taco seasoning mix
24 corn tortillas

In a skillet, brown ground beef; drain. Add 1 cup chile sauce and seasoning. Simmer 5 minutes. For each flauta, fry 2 tortillas in hot oil a few seconds on each side to soften, or place them all in a plastic bag and microwave until steamy. Drain if fried. Lay 2 tortillas flat and overlapping about 2 inches. Spoon 1 to 2 tablespoons of meat lengthwise near one side of the overlapped tortillas. Roll tortillas tightly around filling and secure with toothpicks. Fry in 1-inch hot oil until flauta is crisp. Drain on paper towels and serve with chile sauce. Makes 12, to serve 4 to 6 people.

Variation: Pour puréed avocado over the flautas for a rich colorful topping. Cooked shredded chicken can be substituted for beef.

Tostadas

Essentially, flat tacos without meat.

corn tortillas, fried in oil or heated
     in a 350° oven till crisp
refried beans
finely chopped tomato
grated cheese

finely chopped lettuce
diced green chiles (optional)
black olives (optional)
guacamole (optional)
sour cream

Spread the beans onto the tortillas first and then layer with goodies. The basic
Tostada consists of tortilla, beans, lettuce, tomato and cheese. Go as far as you like!
Add on!

Note: Abuela dice (grandmother says): When frying tortillas, place a copper penny
in the oil and the tortillas will be real crispy.

Taco Salad

1 lb. ground beef
1/2 clove garlic, crushed
1 4-oz. can chopped mild green chiles
1 16-oz. can tomatoes, undrained
1 tsp. salt
1/8 tsp. pepper

1 head iceberg lettuce torn into
　　bite-size pieces
4 oz. Cheddar cheese, grated
6 oz. fried tortilla chips, crushed
1/2 cup chopped green onion
1 tomato, sliced

Sauté beef and garlic until beef is browned. Drain. Add green chiles, canned tomatoes, salt and pepper and mix well. Cook over low heat uncovered for 30 minutes. Just before serving, arrange lettuce, cheese, chips and green onion in a chilled salad bowl. Add meat mixture and toss lightly. Garnish with sliced tomato and serve immediately. This is a good main course luncheon salad.

Chicken Tacos

2 lbs. chicken
1 small onion, chopped
1 to 2 cloves garlic, minced
salt and pepper
taco shells, heated according to
      package directions

shredded lettuce
chopped tomatoes
chopped onion
grated Cheddar cheese
sour cream
guacamole

Stew chicken, either whole or cut up, in a small amount of water. Add onion and garlic, salt and pepper and stew until chicken is very tender and remove bones. Shred chicken. Prepare taco shells, shredded lettuce, chopped tomatoes, onions, cheese, sour cream and guacamole for topping. Filling taco shells with chicken, top with remaining ingredients and enjoy.

Chimichangas

(chim-ee-CHON-gahs)

1 lb. ground beef
10-oz. can tomatoes and green chiles
1 1/4-oz. pkg. taco seasoning mix
12 8-inch flour tortillas
3 cups shredded lettuce

3 cups grated Cheddar cheese
1/2 cup sliced green onion
1 1/2 cups cooked red chile sauce
(commercial or one of the cooked
sauces from this book, your
choice of "heat")

In a skillet, brown ground beef. Drain. Add tomatoes-and-green-chiles and seasoning. Simmer 5 minutes. Spoon 3 tablespoons of meat near one edge of a tortilla. Fold nearest edge over meat; fold both ends in like an envelope. Roll tortilla and secure with toothpicks. Fry in 1-inch hot oil until golden on each side. Drain on paper towels and keep warm. To serve, top each chimichanga with lettuce, cheese, onion and chile sauce. Makes 12.

Variations: Chimichangas can also be made with roast pork or cooked chicken.

Quesadillas

(kay-sah-DEE-yahs)
Grilled Cheese Sandwiches

corn tortillas - 2 to 4 per person
refried beans (optional)

grated or sliced Cheddar cheese
red or green chile sauce, your choice
vegetable oil

Cover half of each tortilla with a layer of refried beans, a layer of cheese and about 2 teaspoonfuls of chile sauce. Heat a griddle or large frying pan to quite hot (not the hottest possible.) Add a generous amount of oil for each batch of quesadillas. Place as many quesadillas on the griddle as it will hold, and as tortillas are softened by the hot oil, gently fold the bare half over the cheese half. When cheese starts to melt, flip quesadillas over, cook briefly, and remove to drain on paper towels. Serve hot. **Variations:** Are endless.

Vegetable Soft Tacos

1 yellow squash, sliced
1 zucchini, sliced
1/2 green pepper, diced
2 medium-sized carrots, sliced thin
1 cup broccoli flowerets
1/2 head cauliflower, broken into
    flowerets
1 cup grated Cheddar cheese

1 cup shredded lettuce
1/2 cup sliced black olives (optional)
1/2 cup fresh or canned mushrooms
    (optional)
1/4 cup onions, diced (optional)
flour tortillas, warmed
Ranch dressing
picante sauce

Place squash, zucchini, green pepper, carrots, broccoli, and cauliflower in a steamer and cook until tender. While steaming, prepare remaining ingredients. When vegetables are steamed, create a buffet line of all ingredients, building a taco on a large soft flour tortilla. Top with Ranch Dressing and picante sauce. Roll up and fold ends. Eat it out-of-hand or off a plate if you prefer.

Black Bean & Beef Burritos

1 lb. ground beef
1 10-oz jar hot green chile salsa
1 15-oz. can condensed black bean
    soup (or 1 1-lb. can refried
    pinto beans)

oil
4 large or 8 small flour tortillas
1/2 lb. sharp white Cheddar cheese,
    grated
1 whole tomato
1/4 large head of lettuce, shredded

Brown beef in skillet and add generous amount of salsa. Cover and simmer 20 minutes. In another skillet, fry black bean soup with a small amount of oil. On a flat flour tortilla, combine meat and refried beans, and top with a good amount of shredded cheese. Roll up and place on a microwave-safe plate or casserole. Top with more salsa. Microwave 30 to 45 seconds each. Serve with tomato and lettuce garnish.

85

Sausage and Bean Burritos

3/4 lb. chorizo, casing removed, and
    crumbled (Mexican sausage)
1 medium-sized onion
1 cup picante sauce
1 tsp. ground cumin
1 16-oz. can pinto or red kidney beans,
    rinsed and drained

10 flour tortillas, heated
1 1/2 cups grated Monterey Jack or
    Cheddar cheese
chopped tomato and avocado
shredded lettuce
ripe olive slices

Cook chorizo sausage well with onion; drain. Stir in picante sauce and cumin; simmer 5 minutes or until most of the liquid has evaporated. Stir in beans. For each burrito, spoon generously 1/3 cup sausage mixture in the center of each tortilla. Top with 2 tablespoons cheese. Add tomato, avocado, lettuce and olives as desired. Fold tortilla over one end of filling and roll. Serve with additional picante sauce. Makes 5 servings.

Vegetable Burritos

1/2 onion, chopped
2 slices turkey bologna or turkey
      pastrami, cut into strips (optional)
1/2 to 1 cup mild red chile sauce
few dashes of Worcestershire sauce
1 stalk broccoli, cut into thin spears
oil

1 carrot, cut into long slivers
1 zucchini, cut into long spears
1/2 to 1 cup refried beans
thin spears of mild pickles (optional)
1/4 lb. Cheddar cheese, grated or
      thinly sliced
6 10-inch flour tortillas

Sauté onion in vegetable oil in a large skillet. Add bologna or pastrami strips. When onion and meat are just browned, add chile sauce, Worcestershire sauce, and vegetables. Steam covered, until vegetables are crisp-tender.

(continued)

Vegetable Burritos *(continued)*

Add a little water if necessary to help steam. On each flour tortilla, spread a strip of refried beans. Place vegetables and meat mixture over beans. Add cheese and pickle. Roll up tortillas, tucking in ends. Wrap individually in plastic wrap and microwave on high 45 seconds. Serve with lettuce and tomatoes if desired. Garnish with salsa or guacamole. Two generous servings.

Enchanted Sour Cream Chicken Enchiladas

2 cups chicken, cooked and cut up
1 cup sour cream
1/8 tsp. salt
dash pepper
12 5-inch corn tortillas

4 oz. canned chopped green chiles, drained
2 cups grated Monterey Jack cheese
lettuce, shredded
tomatoes, chopped

Combine chicken, sour cream, salt and pepper. Quickly fry 1 tortilla at a time in hot oil to soften. Spoon a heaping tablespoon of chicken mixture onto each tortilla, spread down the center and roll up tortilla. Place seam side down in greased 13x9x2-inch baking dish. When all tortillas are filled and rolled, sprinkle the green chiles over all and top with cheese. Bake at 400° for 12 to 15 minutes or until cheese is melted and enchiladas are hot. Serve 2 to 3 enchiladas on a plate and surround with lettuce and tomatoes. Top with your choice of guacamole or sour cream or both. Serves 4 to 6.

Basic Enchilada Information

Enchiladas are corn tortillas wrapped around a filling of beef, chicken or cheese, baked smothered in chile sauce (red or green) and topped with more cheese and onion (chopped Spanish or diced green onion). The meats are often cooked in a chile sauce and sauce is inside as well as on top. Flat enchiladas are fried corn tortillas layered with the same fillings and toppings. Tortillas can be of yellow, white or blue corn, rolled or flat. Fillings can be almost anything. You can use different onions and chile sauces inside and over the enchiladas. Variations are almost endless.

Frying a corn tortilla

Basic Enchiladas

Three Enchilada Fillings:
1) Beef or pork, cooked in the Basic Red Sauce until very tender.
2) Green Chile Stew.
3) Grated cheese and Basic Red Sauce with diced onions (optional).

Toppings for any filling:
1) Basic Red Sauce or any cooked red sauce.
2) Green Chile Sauce or Green Chile Stew.
3) Cheese and onion.
4) Sour cream.

Roll or layer filling in tortillas, top with a topping and bake on individual plates, in a casserole or large baking pans for a crowd. Bake or microwave until cheese melts and enchiladas are hot through.

A Myriad of Enchilada Fillings

To give your enchiladas a distinctly late 20th century flavor.

Avocado Cashew Enchilada Filling

2 ripe avocados, peeled, pitted and
    mashed
4 scallions, minced
1/3 cup sour cream or plain yogurt

4 to 6 Tbs. lemon juice
1 cup toasted cashews, finely chopped
1 clove garlic, pressed
1 1/2 Tbs. parsley

Combine the avocados and lemon juice and mix until smooth. Add remaining ingredients. Serves 4.

Cream Cheese Enchilada Filling

8-oz. pkg. cream cheese, softened
    (try Neufchâtel for variety)
1 cup finely chopped green pepper

4 scallions, minced
1/2 cup each green and black olives
1/3 cup raisins
dash cayenne

Beat cream cheese until creamy, add other ingredients in order, one by one. Blend until smooth. Serves 4.

Egg-Plus Enchilada Filling

4 hard-cooked eggs, finely chopped
1 cup minced onion

1 lb. Monterey Jack cheese
1 1/2 cups black olives
salt and pepper to taste

Combine all ingredients and mix well. Serves 4.

Spicy Zucchini Enchilada Filling

3 Tbs. vegetable oil
3 cloves garlic, pressed
1 cup finely chopped onion
1 cup finely chopped green pepper
2 1/2 cups finely chopped zucchini

1 cup grated sharp Cheddar cheese
1/2 tsp. cumin
1/2 tsp. basil
1/4 tsp. cayenne
1/4 tsp. fresh ground black pepper

Sauté garlic and onion in oil until tender. Add green pepper, zucchini and seasonings and mix well. Do not over cook, cook just until color changes to bright green. Stir in cheese and take off the stove to allow mixture to cool. Fill enchiladas. Serves 4.

Eggs

Animal petroglyphs

Sometimes I go about pitying myself
and all the time I am being carried
on great winds across the sky.
—*Indian Chant*

Baked Chile Rellenos

(ray-YEN-nos)

Green Chile Quiche

8 to 10 long green chiles, mild to hot
10 oz. Monterey Jack cheese, grated
6 eggs, well beaten

2 Tbs. butter, melted
1/2 tsp. salt
1/2 tsp. pepper
1/2 tsp. cumin

Roast, peel and seed chiles; or use canned large whole green chiles drained. Layer chiles alternately with grated cheese in buttered 1 1/2-quart casserole. Mix eggs, butter, salt, pepper and cumin; pour this mixture over chiles and cheese. Bake at 350° for 35 to 40 minutes.

Variations: Can be doubled for a delicious brunch or supper, or baked in a 9x13-inch pan, cut into 1-inch squares and served as an appetizer. Sharp Cheddar may be substituted for the Monterey Jack. Paprika can be used for color.

Mexican Quiche Without Crust

2 cups chopped ham
16 oz. small curd cottage cheese
1 pkg. frozen chopped spinach,
    thawed and drained
6 eggs, beaten

1/2 cup melted margarine or butter
6 Tbs. flour
12 oz. Cheddar cheese, grated
8 oz. mushrooms, sliced
1/2 onion, chopped
6 to 8 oz. chopped green chiles

Mix ingredients and transfer to a 9x13-inch casserole or quiche pan. Bake at 350° for 1 hour. Let stand for 10 minutes before cutting. Serves 8 to 12 people.

Huevos Rancheros

(WAY-vohs ron-CHAIR-os)
Ranch Country Eggs

For each serving:

2 corn tortillas	1 oz. Monterey Jack cheese, grated
2 to 4 Tbs. refried beans	2 eggs, fried to order
	red chile salsa

On a microwave-safe (or ovenproof) plate, place 1 corn tortilla (still frozen is fine); spread on a thick layer of refried beans, top with cheese, then the other tortilla. Cover tightly with plastic wrap and microwave on high about 1 minute, or until cheese melts and tortillas are soft. Remove from microwave and leave covered until eggs are ready. Place eggs on tortillas and top with salsa to taste. Pan-fried potato cubes are an excellent accompaniment.

Breakfast Burritos

Breakfast burritos are popular at the Albuquerque Balloon Fiesta in October, where everyone gets up before dawn to watch 500 to 600 hot-air balloons ascend.

flour tortilla	scrambled egg
2 strips bacon, fried	shredded Monterey Jack cheese
	red or green salsa to taste

Roll everything up in the flour tortilla.

Variations: Cooked crumbled or sliced chorizo may be substituted for bacon for a spicier burrito. Fried, grated or cubed potatoes can be added.

Spanish Egg Breakfast Casserole

10 eggs
1/2 cup flour
1 tsp. baking powder
1/2 stick margarine

2 small cans chopped green chiles
1 pint cottage cheese
1 lb. Cheddar cheese, grated
1 lb. sausage, cooked and crumbled

Mix all ingredients together. Pour into a greased 9x13-inch baking pan. Bake 15 minutes at 400°. Reduce heat to 350° for 35 minutes. Cut into squares to serve. Leftovers are good heated in the microwave.

Casseroles and Other Main Dishes

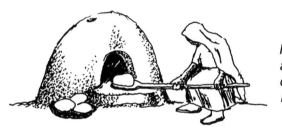

*Horno,
adobe baking oven
of Moorish-Spanish-
Pueblo Indian usage*

Cuando el horno está caliente, poca lena necesita.
When the oven is hot you don't need very much wood.

Chicken Sopa

Sopa is something served in a bowl, anything from a thick stew to bread pudding.

oil
2 medium-sized onions, chopped
12 oz. chopped mild green chiles
5 cups diced cooked chicken
18 corn tortillas, fried until crisp
13 oz. cream of celery soup

13 oz. cream of mushroom soup
24 oz. canned tomatoes, drained
 and chopped
3 cups water (you may include juice from
 tomatoes in this measurement)
10 oz. Monterey Jack cheese, grated
10 oz. Cheddar cheese, grated

Sauté onions and chiles until tender. Add diced chicken. Prepare soups using tomatoes and water. In 9x13-inch pan or casserole, alternate layers of tortillas, chicken, soups and cheeses. Bake 45 to 60 minutes at 350°. Top with equal amounts of grated Monterey Jack and Cheddar cheese. Return to oven till melted. Serve hot. Serves 12 to 13 people.

Tamale Pie

2 Tbs. salad oil
1 medium-sized green pepper, diced
1 large onion, diced
2 tsp. salt
2 lbs. lean ground beef

1/4 tsp. pepper
1-lb. can tomatoes
1 Tbs. chili powder (or less)
1 10 to 12-oz. pkg. corn muffin mix
1 cup evaporated milk
3/4 cup grated cheese

Sauté green pepper and onion in oil with beef and seasonings. Brown and drain. Add tomatoes. Simmer 30 minutes. Prepare corn muffin mix with milk. Place meat mixture on bottom of 8x12-inch baking dish. Spread muffin mix on top and sprinkle cheese on top of that. Bake about 20 to 25 minutes in a 375° oven until corn topping is done and brown.

Variations: Mild red chile sauce can be substituted for part of tomatoes.

New Mexican Pepper Casserole

6 medium-sized bell peppers of
    various colors, sliced in thin strips
1 1/2 cups finely chopped onion
2 Tbs. butter
2 Tbs. oil
3 cloves of garlic, pressed
1 tsp. dry cumin

1/2 tsp. dry mustard
1/2 tsp. chili powder
salt to taste
4 large eggs
1 1/2 cups sour cream
1/2 lb. Cheddar cheese, thinly sliced
paprika

Heat butter and oil in a skillet and sauté onions, garlic and spices. When onions are clear, add sliced peppers and sauté for 10 minutes. In a deep buttered casserole, layer half the pepper mixture and half the cheese, repeat. Whisk together the eggs and sour cream. Pour over layered cheese and peppers. Sprinkle with paprika and bake at 375° for 30 minutes covered, 15 minutes uncovered. Serves 6.

Chile Rellenos
Stuffed Chiles

8 fresh green chile peppers roasted and peeled (do not remove stems) or 8 canned whole chiles

8 strips 1x2 1/2-inches long of Monterey Jack or white cheese

salt to taste

To roast green chiles: Place on charcoal grill, or in oven broiler. When skin is brown and blistered on one side, turn chiles with tongs. Continue turning, roasting and blistering, until skin has lost its fresh green color but is not too burned. Put roasted chiles immediately into a plastic bag to continue to steam and cook. Remove skins from pulp, wearing rubber gloves if the chiles are a hot variety. Try to keep chiles whole. Leave the stems on; it's traditional.

(continued)

Chile Rellenos   *(continued)*

Make a slit in chile below stem just large enough to insert strip of cheese, roll in flour, then dip in the following batter.

Batter for Chile Rellenos:

1/2 cup flour	1 cup milk
pancake or biscuit mix	1 egg

To flour add enough pancake or biscuit mix to make 2/3 cup. Add milk and egg. Beat until smooth. Dip cheese-stuffed chiles in batter and fry in about 1 inch of hot fat until golden brown. Serve hot.

Beef Fajitas
(fah-HEE-tahs)

Skirt steak is preferred, fajitas are supposed to be stringy and a little chewy. This is also why the meat is sliced with the grain instead of across it.

2 lbs. skirt steaks, sliced with the grain, 1/4 inch thick
3 cloves garlic, chopped
1/2 cup Worcestershire sauce
2 Tbs. liquid smoke
1 Tbs. ground cumin
dash black pepper

1 12-oz. can beer
1 onion, chopped
2 tomatoes, chopped
1 green bell pepper, chopped
flour tortillas
guacamole
green chile salsa

(continued)

Beef Fajitas   *(continued)*

Combine first seven ingredients in a glass or steel bowl, cover and refrigerate 12 to 24 hours. (To do it faster, use instant meat tenderizer instead of beer and follow directions on its package.) Drain marinade. In an iron skillet over medium heat, grill meat in olive oil. Remove meat and keep warm. In same pan grill onion, tomatoes and bell pepper in meat juices. Serve meat and vegetables wrapped in a flour tortilla with guacamole and salsa.

Variation: Fajitas can also be made with marinated chicken. Try lime juice, a little red chili powder, liquid smoke and a touch of oregano.

Beef Fajitas

(fah-HEE-tahs)

2 lbs. skirt steak or flank steak
1/2 cup olive oil
1/4 cup tequila
1/4 cup lime or lemon juice
2 cups hickory barbecue sauce
1 can beer

1/8 cup soy sauce
1 Spanish or red onion, sliced in strips
1 green pepper, sliced into strips
    (optional)
Pico de Gallo sauce
flour tortillas, steamed or heated

Combine oil, tequila and juice and marinate meat overnight in the refrigerator. Next day, pour off marinade. Combine barbecue sauce, beer and soy sauce. Slice steak into strips with the grain; marinate at least an hour in barbecue sauce mixture. On a charcoal grill, cook steak strips like a medium steak. When steak is about done, place onion and green pepper right on the meat and cook until done. Serve with Pico de Gallo and roll up in flour tortillas.

109

Pork Chops with Corn Bread Stuffing

1/4 cup butter or margarine
1 small onion, chopped
1/2 cup chopped celery
1 1/2 cups water

1 6-oz. pkg. corn bread stuffing mix
6 thick rib pork chops, with a pocket
    cut in each
2 Tbs. vegetable oil
3/4 cup chicken broth

In a saucepan, melt butter. Sauté onion and celery until just tender. Stir in water and seasonings from stuffing mix. Cover and simmer 5 minutes. Remove from heat. Stir in stuffing mix. Stuff pork chops; secure with wooden toothpicks. In a large skillet, heat oil. Brown chops on both sides. Place in a 12x8-inch baking pan. Cover and bake at 350° for 30 minutes. Add broth. Bake, uncovered, 30 minutes longer or until tender.

Pork and Beans

3 cups dried pinto beans
6 to 8 cups water
1/2 lb. slab of bacon or ham hocks,
    cut up
1 medium-sized onion, chopped

2 cloves garlic, mashed
1 6-oz. can tomato paste
1 1/2 Tbs. chile powder
1 tsp. salt
1 tsp. cumin seed
1/2 tsp. marjoram

In a Crockpot, cover beans with water and soak overnight. Next day add remaining ingredients and cook on low for 8 to 10 hours. Serves 8. Serve with corn bread.

Variations: Add a can of beer to the recipe and call it "Drunken Beans", or add a diced carrot, or use black beans, which taste wonderful in this.

Mexican Manicotti in Microwave

1/2 lb. lean ground beef
1 cup refried beans
1 tsp. dried oregano
1/2 tsp. ground cumin
8 manicotti shells

1 1/4 cups water
1 8-oz. can picante or taco sauce
8-oz. carton of sour cream
1/4 cup sliced black olives
1/4 cup green onions, chopped
1/2 cup grated Monterey Jack cheese

Combine ground beef, refried beans, oregano and cumin; mix well. Fill uncooked manicotti shells with meat mixture. Arrange in 10x6x2-inch baking dish. Combine water and picante sauce. Pour over manicotti shells. Cover with vented plastic wrap. Microwave on high for 10 minutes, giving the dish a half-turn once. Using tongs, turn shells over. Microwave on medium 17 to 19 minutes or until pasta is tender, giving dish half turn once during cooking. Combine sour cream, green onion and olives. Spoon down center of casserole. Top with cheese. Microwave uncovered on high 2 to 3 minutes or until cheese melts. Makes 4 servings.

Uncle Bill's Smoked Sausage

10 lbs. ground venison and lean
    ground beef, mixed
5 tsp. mustard seed
5 tsp. crushed, cracked peppercorns

1 Tbs. garlic salt
5 tsp. liquid smoke
5 tsp. black pepper
10 tsp. Morton's Quick-Cure salt

Mix ingredients together, kneading well. Refrigerate 24 hours; mix again. Refrigerate another 24 hours. Shape into 12 rolls—2x10 inches each. Place on broiler type pan with tray to drain, not touching each other. Bake 10 hours at 150° uncovered. Wipe with paper towel before wrapping and storing; refrigerate for at least 48 hours before eating. Makes its own casing while cooking.

Arroz con Pollo

(ar-ROZ cohn PO-yo)
Rice with Chicken

This is a seasoned chicken and rice dish—a flavorful skillet supper all cooking in the same pan!

1 frying chicken, cut up
1/2 cup flour
1 Tbs. chili powder
salt and pepper to taste
vegetable oil

1/2 cup finely chopped green pepper
1/2 cup finely chopped onion
1 garlic clove, minced or pressed
2 cups water
1 16-oz. can tomatoes, chopped
1 cup uncooked regular rice

(continued)

Arroz con Pollo   *(continued)*

Rinse chicken under running water, removing excess fat; drain. Combine flour, chili powder, salt and pepper; dredge chicken pieces in this mixture. Brown evenly in a large skillet in a small amount of oil. Remove chicken from pan. Add green pepper, onion and garlic to pan of chicken drippings. Sauté until tender. Stir in water, tomatoes and rice. Arrange chicken over rice mixture. Cover and simmer 45 minutes or until chicken is tender. Makes 4 servings. If desired, use more tomatoes and less water.

Mexican-Style Chicken Kiev

4 whole chicken breasts, deboned
1 7-oz. can green chiles
1/4 lb. Monterey Jack cheese
1/2 cup fine dry bread crumbs
1/4 cup grated Parmesan cheese

1 tsp. chili powder
1/2 tsp. garlic salt
1/4 tsp. ground cumin
1/4 tsp. pepper
6 Tbs. butter or margarine, melted

Spicy Tomato Sauce:
1 15-oz. can tomato sauce
1/2 tsp. ground cumin

1/3 cup sliced green onion
salt and pepper to taste

Pound chicken breasts between two pieces of waxed paper until each is about 1/4 inch thick.

(continued)

Mexican-Style Chicken Kiev   *(continued)*

Slit the green chiles in half lengthwise and remove seeds, then cut into 8 equal pieces. Cut the cheese into 8 fingers about 1 1/2x1/2-inches. Combine crumbs, Parmesan, chili powder, garlic salt, cumin and pepper. Lay a piece of green chile and a finger of Monterey Jack on each of the chicken pieces. Roll up to enclose the filling, tuck ends under. Dip bundles in melted butter, drain briefly, then roll in the crumb mixture to coat evenly. Place bundles seam-side down, without sides touching, in a 9x13-inch baking dish. Drizzle remaining butter over all. Cover and chill for at least 4 hours or overnight. To serve, uncover and bake at 400° for 20 minutes or until chicken is no longer pink when slashed. Transfer to serving plate and pass the sauce. Serves 8.

Spicy Tomato Sauce: Heat the tomato sauce, cumin and green onion until hot. Season to taste with salt and pepper.

Carne Adovada

(CAR-nay ah-doh-VAH-da)

Marinated Meat

Chile is high in vitamin A and also is an anti-oxidant. Indians used chile pulp to preserve meat before refrigeration.

8 oz. red chiles	2 tsp. ground cumin
2 to 3 cups water	1/4 cup wine vinegar
4 cloves garlic, minced	2 to 3 lbs. lean pork, trimmed of fat and
1 Tbs. oregano	cut into 1x1/2-inch strips

Combine all the ingredients, except pork, to make a thick marinade. Marinate pork at least 24 hours. Drain and bake pork at 325° for 1 hour or until tender and done. Serves 4 to 6.

Serving Suggestions: Serve with Spanish rice and refried beans. In a flour tortilla it is a Carne Adovada Burrito. Diced potatoes and onions may be added before baking.

Avocado Stacks

1 15-oz. can chili with beans

1 12-oz. can Mexican-style corn, drained

8 oz. Cheddar cheese, grated, divided

1 4-oz. can chopped green chiles, drained

1/2 tsp. salt

12 corn tortillas

cooking oil

2 avocados, pitted, peeled and cut into crescents

bottled taco sauce

sour cream (optional)

chopped tomato (optional)

Preheat oven to 350°. In a bowl, combine chili, corn, 1 cup cheese, green chiles and salt; toss lightly to mix. Dip tortillas, one at a time, in hot oil for a few seconds on each side until limp. Drain on paper towels. Spread chili mixture on top of a tortilla; top with another tortilla and sprinkle with some of the remaining cheese. Repeat with remaining tortillas. Heat tortillas in oven for 10 minutes, or until heated through. Top with avocado crescents and taco sauce. Garnish with sour cream and chopped tomato. Makes 6 avocado stacks.

Blue Polenta Pizza

Crust:

1 cup blue corn meal (coarse polenta
    grind is best)
1 cup cold water

1 tsp. salt
2 cups boiling water
1/3 cup grated Parmesan cheese
1 egg

Topping:

1 1/2 cups grated mozzarella cheese
1/2 cup thinly sliced onions
1/2 cup minced green pepper
1/2 cup minced green chiles
1 Tbs. olive oil

dash of oregano
dash garlic powder
dash black pepper
1 large tomato, sliced
grated Parmesan cheese

(continued)

Blue Polenta Pizza   *(continued)*

Crust: Combine corn meal, cold water, and salt. Stir into boiling water; cook for five minutes until thick. Remove from heat and add cheese. Beat a spoonful of hot polenta into egg, then beat the egg mixture back into polenta. Butter a 9-inch pie pan. Pat the polenta into the pie pan using a spatula. Let stand several hours, uncovered, until surface is dry. Bake at 350° for 45 minutes.

Topping: Sauté onion and green pepper in olive oil until tender. Add spices. Sprinkle two-thirds of the mozzarella onto the baked crust. Spread the sautéed vegetables over the cheese. Arrange slices of tomato over the vegetables. Top with remaining mozzarella and a little Parmesan. Broil until brown and bubbly. Serve hot.

Fish Vera Cruz, New Mexico Style

2 large fillets of white fish, cod,
    red snapper or bluefish
1/2 cup butter
1/4 cup lemon juice
1/4 cup olive oil
1 onion, chopped
1 bell pepper, chopped

1/4 tsp. ground dried rosemary or
    a pinch of fresh rosemary
1 1-lb. can whole tomatoes, drained
1 8-oz. jar hot green chili sauce or
    hot picante sauce
salt and pepper
lemon pepper

Melt butter in baking dish. Add fillets, lemon juice, salt, pepper and lemon pepper to taste. Bake at 350° for 15 to 20 minutes or until fish flakes easily. In a large skillet, sauté onion and bell pepper in olive oil until soft. Add rosemary, salsa and tomatoes. Simmer 15 to 20 minutes, chopping tomatoes as you stir, until it's not watery and liquid is condensed. Place fish fillets on serving plate and pour sauce over fish.

Barbecue in Cups

3/4 lb. ground beef
1/2 cup barbecue sauce
1 Tbs. minced onion

2 Tbs. brown sugar
1 8-oz. can of 12 biscuits
3/4 cup shredded Cheddar cheese

Heat oven to 400°. Brown ground beef; drain. Add barbecue sauce, onion and brown sugar. Separate biscuit dough into 12 biscuits. Place 1 biscuit in each of 12 ungreased muffin cups, pressing dough up sides to the edge of cup. Spoon the meat mixture into cups. Sprinkle each with cheese. Bake 10 to 12 minutes or until golden brown.

Side Dishes

Las peñas con pan son menos.
With bread, worries are less.

La esperanza es la última que muere.
Hope is the last thing that dies.

Traditional Spanish Rice

2 Tbs. chopped onion
1 clove garlic, minced
1/2 cup chopped celery

3 Tbs. shortening or olive oil
1 cup uncooked rice
3 cups canned tomatoes
salt and pepper to taste

Cook onion, garlic and celery in shortening or olive oil. Add rice and brown lightly. Add remaining ingredients. Cook covered over low heat. After 15 minutes, check; add water if necessary. Cook until rice is tender and liquid is absorbed. Serves 6.

Avocado Salad

This is a variation from South America.

1 large avocado	4 to 6 Tbs. lemon juice
2 large tomatoes	pinch salt
1 green pepper	1 tsp. chili powder
1 8-oz. pkg. cream cheese	ground paprika
6 Tbs. vegetable oil	lettuce leaves

Peel and pit the avocado, and cut into thick slices. Chop tomatoes and pepper and mix with avocado. Melt the cream cheese over low heat in a pan and mix with oil and lemon juice, salt and chili powder to make a thick sauce. Line a dish with lettuce leaves and sprinkle with paprika. Spoon salad on this in the shape of a pyramid and pour sauce over it. Serves 2 to 4.

Corn Relish

1/4 cup white vinegar
2 17-oz. cans whole kernel corn,
    drained
1/4 cup light corn syrup
1 small onion, chopped

1 cup chopped bell peppers,
    red or green
2 Tbs. chopped parsley
1/4 cup corn oil
1/4 tsp. salt

In a large bowl stir together all ingredients. Toss to coat well. Cover, refrigerate several hours or overnight. If desired drain before serving. Makes about 4 cups.

Variation: Add jalapeños if you like it a little spicy.

Calico Corn

1/2 cup sliced fresh mushrooms
1/3 cup chopped green pepper
1/3 cup chopped onion
2 Tbs. butter

1 16-oz. can whole kernel corn, drained
1 2-oz. jar pimientos, drained and diced
2 Tbs. celery flakes
dash cayenne or hot pepper sauce

Place mushrooms, green pepper, onion and butter in 1 1/2-quart glass or ceramic dish. Microwave uncovered 1 to 2 minutes or until tender. Add remaining ingredients. Microwave covered 1 to 3 minutes or until heated through, stirring once during cooking.

Calabacitas Sureñas

Zucchini, Southern Mexico Style

6 medium-sized zucchini, sliced
    (yellow and green mixed)
2 onions, sliced in rings
3 tomatoes, chopped
1 clove garlic, minced

2 sweet green peppers, jalepeños, or
    1 can hot green chiles, chopped
1/4 lb. pork, diced and fried
salt and pepper to taste
1 cup grated cheese

Layer zucchini, onions, tomatoes, garlic and peppers in microwave dish. Cook 12 to 16 minutes at high power. Add pork and season with salt and pepper. Before serving sprinkle with grated cheese. Heat 1 minute, or until cheese is melted. Serves 6.

Calabacitas

Squash Casserole

2 scallop squashes, sliced
2 yellow squashes, sliced
2 zucchini, sliced
2 cups corn
1/2 onion, chopped
1 clove garlic, minced

chile to taste (red chile powder or
   chopped green chiles)
1/4 cup piñon nut meats (pine nuts)
10 blue corn tortillas
2 cups cream of chicken soup
1 lb. Cheddar cheese, grated

Sauté squash and corn in oil over high heat until browned. Add garlic and onion to cook but not brown. Stir in chile to taste. In 8x10-inch baking pan, layer vegetables, piñon nuts, and tortillas, pour soup over, then sprinkle grated cheese on top. Bake at 325° for 30 minutes. Serves 8.

Green Chile Cheese Spoonbread

1/2 cup yellow corn meal
2 Tbs. butter
1/2 tsp. salt
1 1/2 tsp. baking powder
pepper to taste

1 cup boiling water
3 large eggs
1/2 cup milk
1 4-oz. can chopped green chiles
1 cup shredded Monterey Jack cheese

Preheat oven to 400° and generously butter a 1-quart baking dish. Blend the first 6 ingredients in a food processor or blender for about 5 seconds, stopping at least once to scrape down the sides of the bowl. Add eggs and milk and blend a few seconds more to mix thoroughly. Pour 1/2 of the batter into a baking dish. Spoon green chiles evenly over the batter and sprinkle most of the cheese, reserving a small amount of cheese for topping. Pour remaining batter over the chiles and cheese layer. Sprinkle remaining cheese over the top and bake for about 20 minutes. This is a soft bread so it must be served with a spoon as a side dish or as a main dish with beans and salad or fruit. Serves 4.

Indian Pudding

3 cups milk
6 Tbs. molasses
6 Tbs. corn meal
1 egg, slightly beaten

1/4 cup sugar
2 Tbs. butter
1/2 tsp. ground ginger
1/2 tsp. ground cinnamon
1/4 tsp. salt

In saucepan combine milk and molasses; stir in corn meal. Cook, stirring constantly, till thick, about 10 minutes. Remove from heat. Combine egg, sugar, butter, ginger, cinnamon and salt. Gradually stir in hot corn meal mixture. Bake, uncovered, in a 1-quart casserole at 300° for 1 1/2 hours. Makes 6 servings.

Corn Pudding

Very much like Native Americans make.

1 can cream style corn
3/4 cup milk
2 eggs
1 can whole kernel corn, drained

1/3 cup salad oil
1 cup corn meal
1/2 tsp. baking soda
1 tsp. salt

Combine first 5 ingredients, mix well. Add remaining ingredients, blend and pour into a baking dish. Bake at 400° for 45 minutes.

Variations: Add green chiles or grated cheese.

Arroz Dulce

(ar-ROSE DOOL-say)
Sweet Rice Pudding

Corn pudding, from the Native American tradition, is more common in the southern part of New Mexico. This rice pudding is traditional in the North.

1 cup uncooked regular rice
2 cups water
1 tsp. salt
2 cups evaporated milk
3/4 cup sugar

3 eggs, separated
1 cup raisins
3/4 tsp. vanilla
1/4 tsp. cinnamon
1/4 tsp. nutmeg (optional)

Place rice, water and salt into a large saucepan. Bring to a boil and cover, continue cooking, over low heat until water is absorbed. Stir together the milk, sugar and egg yolks and add this to the rice. Stir in raisins, vanilla and cinnamon, and simmer 5 minutes. Remove from heat. Beat egg whites until stiff and fold into rice. Turn into serving dish and chill. Garnish with nutmeg if desired.

Calabaza
Sensational Squash

4 cups cooked and mashed pumpkin
    or other winter squash,
1 1/2 cups chopped red and green
    peppers,
1 cup chopped onion
3 cloves of garlic, pressed
2 cups corn (fresh or frozen)

4 eggs, beaten
2 Tbs. oil
1 tsp. ground cumin
1 tsp. chili powder
1/2 tsp. ground coriander
1 tsp. salt
dash each of cayenne and black pepper
1 cup grated Cheddar cheese

Sauté garlic, onions and spices in oil until clear. Add peppers and salt and cook over medium heat until slightly tender, about 5 minutes. Add mixture to squash. Fold in corn and eggs and mix well. Spread into 2-quart buttered casserole and top with cheese. Bake covered at 350° for 20 minutes, then uncover and bake 15 minutes longer. Serves 4 to 6.

Navajo Fry Bread

1 pkg. dry yeast	3 Tbs. sugar
6 cups flour	2 1/2 tsp. salt
2 1/2 cups warm water	3 Tbs. shortening

Sprinkle yeast over flour in large bowl. Heat water (don't boil). Stir in sugar, salt, shortening. Let cool to lukewarm. With fork stir liquid mixture into flour. Knead well. Let rise for 30 minutes. Pinch off a dough ball about the size of a lemon. Roll out thin. Fry in an 8-inch skillet in only enough fat to cover bottom of pan. Drain and salt lightly. Will serve 8. Leftovers can be reheated and enjoyed.

Variation: The Navajo Taco is made by layering meat, beans, lettuce, tomatoes and cheese onto fry bread.

136

Papas Chorreadas

(POP-ahs cho-ray-AH-das)
Potatoes with spiced cheese, tomato and onion sauce

2 Tbs. butter
4 green onions, cut into 1-inch lengths
    or 1/2 cup finely chopped onion
5 tomatoes, peeled, seeded, and
    coarsely chopped
5 green chiles, chopped
1/2 cup heavy cream

1 tsp. finely chopped fresh cilantro
1/4 tsp. dried oregano
pinch ground cumin
1/2 tsp. salt
freshly ground black pepper
1 cup grated colby-longhorn cheese
8 large potatoes, peeled and boiled

In a heavy skillet over moderate heat, heat the butter, add onions and cook for 5 minutes until soft but not brown. Add tomatoes and chiles; cook stirring for 5 minutes. Add cream and spices, and stirring constantly, drop in the cheese. Cook, stirring until cheese melts. The chorreadas sauce is traditionally served over boiled potatoes. Serves 8.

Sopaipillas
Sweet Fried Cakes

4 cups flour
1 tsp. salt
2 tsp. baking powder
4 Tbs. fat (lard or shortening)

4 eggs
1 cup sugar, divided
water or milk
fat for frying
1 tsp. cinnamon

Sift flour with salt and baking powder. Cut fat into flour. Beat eggs, add 1/2 cup sugar, and add to flour mixture. Add enough milk or water to make a dough that is neither stiff or soft. Let dough stand for 1/2 hour. Roll out 1/4-inch thick, cut into 1 1/2-inch squares and fry in deep fat until brown. Mix the remaining sugar and cinnamon. As the sopaipillas are fried, drained and still hot, roll in the sugar-cinnamon mixture.

Easy Sopaipillas

1 can of ready to cook biscuits   oil for deep frying

Roll out each biscuit as large as possible. Cut in half and fry in deep fat. Be sure to turn each to brown on each side. (May have to be held with fork or spatula to brown second side as they puff up.) Serve hot with honey.

Sopaipillas are the bread served with a meal. Drizzled with honey, they are an ideal way to end a heavy spicy meal instead of dessert.

Blue Corn Buttermilk Muffins

1 egg, beaten
1/2 cup brown sugar
1 cup buttermilk
1/3 cup all-purpose flour
2/3 cup blue corn meal

1/2 tsp. salt
1/2 tsp. baking soda
1 1/2 tsp. baking powder
1/2 cup vegetable oil
red raspberry preserves (optional)

Preheat oven to 400°. Beat together egg, sugar and buttermilk. Combine dry ingredients. Add dry mixture to egg mixture, alternating with the oil. Stir or beat with electric mixer until combined; batter will be thin. Fill paper-lined cups about 2/3 full. Spoon in 1/4 teaspoon of preserves into each cup, if desired. Bake at 400° 12 to 14 minutes. Makes 15 muffins.

Confetti Corn Bread

1 cup plus 1 Tbs. yellow corn meal
1 cup all-purpose flour
2 to 4 Tbs. sugar, to taste
1 Tbs. baking powder
1/4 tsp. salt
1/4 tsp. dried oregano, crushed
2 eggs, slightly beaten

1 cup milk
1/4 cup cooking oil
1 4-oz. can chopped green chiles, drained
1 2-oz. jar sliced pimiento, drained and diced
2 Tbs. finely chopped green onion

Grease a 6 1/2-cup (about 8x8-inch) baking pan. Coat with 1 tablespoon of corn meal, set aside. In a mixing bowl, stir together corn meal, flour, sugar, baking powder, salt and oregano. Add eggs, milk and oil. Beat just until combined, do not over beat. Fold in peppers, pimiento and onion. Pour evenly into prepared pan. Bake at 400° until golden brown, about 20 to 25 minutes. Serves 8.

Desserts

Human petroglyphs

¿Qué sabe el burro de chocolate?
What does a burro know about chocolate?

Cuando dos se quieren bien, con uno que coma basta.
When two are in love, if only one eats, it should be sufficient.

Capirotada
Bread Pudding

This is an "old" revised recipe carried through generations. It is "topped" with panocha syrup.

butter
3 eggs, well beaten
4 Tbs. milk
dash salt
1 tsp. ground cinnamon
1/4 tsp. cloves
1/2 tsp. nutmeg
2 Tbs. light brown sugar

8 slices of toasted bread
1 cup diced cheese, colby or longhorn,
    divided
2/3 cup raisins
2/3 cup Spanish peanuts
3/4 cup chopped pecans or almonds
1 medium-sized apple, peeled, cored,
    and diced

(continued)

143

Capirotada *(continued)*

Generously butter a square casserole dish or baking pan. Preheat oven to 375°. In a mixing bowl, combine eggs, milk, salt, cinnamon, cloves, nutmeg, and sugar. Beat until well blended; add 1 to 2 more tablespoons milk if needed for mixing. Place 4 toasted bread slices in buttered baking pan. Bread should fit evenly in pan. Pour half the egg mixture over the bread. Sprinkle with 1/2 each of the cheese, raisins, peanuts, pecans and apple. Add another layer of bread slices and repeat, using the remaining ingredients. Top entire capirotada with Panocha Sauce (recipe found on the next page.) Bake 15 minutes until well heated and cheese is melted. Let cool, cut into squares and serve warm. Serves 4 to 6.

Panocha Syrup

Syrup is delicious when served over Mexican pastries. Panocha can be made into a sauce by using milk instead of water.

2 cups light brown sugar or
    1 1/3 cups Piloncillo (a Mexican
    brown sugar that is sweeter and
    tastier than regular brown sugar)
2 cups water

In a saucepan dissolve sugar in water. Bring to a slow boil, stirring frequently. Cover and simmer for 20 to 25 minutes. Spoon out any crystallized sugar that may form on the sides of the pan or over the syrup. Serve over desired pastry. Makes 1 1/4 cup syrup. Store in an airtight glass jar and refrigerate until ready to use.

Flan
Caramel Custard

Caramel Sauce:
1 cup white sugar

1/3 cup white corn syrup

Flan:
6 eggs
1 cup sugar

3 1/2 cups milk
1 tsp. vanilla

Caramel Sauce: Melt sugar in saucepan over very low heat. Add syrup, mix and pour into bottom of a 1 1/2-inch-deep glass baking dish or equally into 6 custard cups.
Flan: Beat eggs, gradually adding sugar. Mix in milk and vanilla. Pour over the caramel sauce. Bake at 350° for 45 minutes (or less for individual cups) or until firm. Turn out on serving plates. Caramel sauce will cover the custard.

Natillas
Custard

2 cups milk
1 pinch salt
1 tsp. vanilla

3 Tbs. flour
1/2 cup sugar
2 eggs, separated
powdered cinnamon

In medium-sized saucepan warm milk. Beat egg yolks, add sugar, flour and salt. Add to milk. Heat until it boils and thickens. Add vanilla. Beat egg whites until stiff, fold egg mixture into egg whites. Sprinkle top with powdered cinnamon. Serve cold. Serves 3 to 4.

Easy Fresh Apple Cake

2 cups sugar
1 tsp. salt
1 tsp. baking soda
3 cups flour

4 eggs
1 cup oil
2 tsp. vanilla
3 cups chopped apples
1 cup chopped pecans

Sift together dry ingredients. Make a hole in the middle of the dry mixture and add oil, eggs and vanilla. Mix well. Add apples and nuts. Pour into greased 10-inch tube pan or Bundt pan and bake at 350° for about 25 minutes or until cake tests done.

Biscochitos
Anise Seed Cookies

1 lb. butter-flavored Crisco
1 1/2 cups sugar
2 tsp. anise seed
2 eggs, beaten
6 cups flour

3 tsp. baking powder
1 tsp. salt
1/2 cup orange juice
1/4 cup sugar
1 Tbs. cinnamon

Cream Crisco, sugar and anise seed in a large bowl. Add eggs and beat well. Combine flour, baking powder and salt in a large bowl. Alternately add flour mixture and orange juice to creamed mixture until a stiff dough is formed. Knead dough slightly and pat or roll to a 1/4 to 1/2 inch thickness. Cut dough into desired shapes.

(continued)

Biscochitos   *(continued)*

Combine sugar and cinnamon in a small bowl. Dust the top of each cookie with a small amount of the cinnamon-sugar mixture. Bake at 350° for 10 minutes, or until cookies are lightly browned.

Variations: Lard, rather than vegetable shortening, is traditional; 1/4 cup of brandy or more can be substituted for the orange juice. More flour makes them crisper, less flour more melt-in-your-mouth. The fleur-de-lis shape is traditional for these cookies.

Polvorones
Mexican Wedding Cakes

1 cup butter or margarine
1/2 cup sifted powdered sugar
1 tsp. vanilla

2 cups all-purpose flour
1/2 cup finely chopped pecans
1/8 tsp. salt
powdered sugar

Cream butter, the 1/2 cup powdered sugar and vanilla. Combine flour, pecans and salt. Stir into butter mixture. Shape dough into 1-inch balls. Place on ungreased baking sheet. Bake in 325° oven 20 to 25 minutes till lightly browned. Roll warm cookies in powdered sugar. Cool on wire racks, then roll again in powdered sugar. Makes 36.

Santa Fe Brownies

4 squares unsweetened chocolate
1 cup butter or margarine
2 cups sugar
4 eggs

1 cup flour
1/2 tsp. salt
1/2 to 1 cup piñon nuts
1 tsp. vanilla

In a medium-sized pan, melt chocolate and butter together over low heat. Remove from heat and stirring constantly add sugar. Stir well and allow to cool, then beat in the eggs one at a time, beating thoroughly after each. Add flour and salt. Mix well. Add vanilla and nuts. Pour into a greased 9x13-inch pan and bake at 350° for 35 to 45 minutes.

Dulces de Naranja

Mexican Orange Candy

3 cups sugar, divided
1/4 cup boiling water
1 cup evaporated milk

dash salt
2 tsp. grated orange rind
1 cup pecans

Caramelize 1 cup sugar, stirring constantly. When the sugar is melted and golden brown in color, add the boiling water and cook till it becomes a smooth syrup, stirring constantly. Add the rest of the sugar, milk and salt. Cook over medium heat until soft ball stage, or 238° (about 35 minutes). Stir occasionally. Add the orange peel, cool and stir in the nuts. When candy is room temperature, beat till crystalline. Drop from a teaspoon onto waxed paper.

Empanaditas

1 qt. boiling water
2 cups dried peaches, apricots or apples
1/2 cup raisins
2 pkg. prepared pie crust mix

1 cup sugar or less
1 tsp. cinnamon
1/2 tsp. nutmeg
1/4 tsp. salt
1/4 cup piñon nuts (pine nuts)

In a saucepan, cover fruit with boiling water; let stand. Prepare pie crust recipe according to package directions. Roll thin and cover with plastic wrap and keep airtight. Place saucepan of fruit over medium heat, bring to boil and simmer. Stir to keep from sticking. When fruit is tender, add sugar to taste, spices and salt. Cook fruit until soft, adding water only if needed. Drain and mash fruit. Add piñon nuts. Preheat oven to 400°. Cut dough into 4-inch circles with biscuit cutter or knife. Place 1 teaspoon of fruit in the center of each round. Moisten edges with water, fold rounds in half and press edges with fork. Bake on cookie sheets 12 to 14 minutes or until golden. Cool on racks. Makes 20 to 24 empanaditas.

Lemon Cream Pie

Refreshing and light to cool your mouth after a hot New Mexican meal.

1   9-inch graham cracker crust
4 egg yolks
1   14-oz. can sweetened condensed
        milk

1/2 cup lemon juice
few drops of yellow food coloring
whipped topping or whipped cream
lemon slices

Preheat oven to 350°. In a medium-sized bowl, beat egg yolks. Stir in milk, lemon juice and food coloring. Pour into crust and bake 8 minutes. Cool and chill thoroughly. Top with whipped cream and garnish with thinly sliced lemon.

Margarita Pie

Crust:

3/4 cup pretzel crumbs

1/3 cup butter, melted

3 Tbs. sugar

Filling:

1 envelope plain gelatin

1/2 cup lemon juice

4 eggs, separated

1 cup sugar, divided

1/4 tsp. salt

1 tsp. grated lemon rind

1/3 cup tequila

3 Tbs. Triple Sec

Crust: Combine crumbs, butter and sugar. Press into a 9-inch pie plate. Chill.

(continued)

Margarita Pie   *(continued)*

Filling: Sprinkle gelatin over lemon juice; let stand until soft. Beat egg yolks in top of a double boiler. Blend in 1/2 cup sugar, salt and lemon rind. Add gelatin. Cook over boiling water, stirring constantly until thick. Remove from heat and blend in tequila and Triple Sec. Chill. Beat egg whites until foamy; gradually add remaining sugar, continuing to beat until stiff peaks form. Fold in cooked mixture. Spoon into crust; chill. Serves 8.

Tía María Ice Cream Shake

You can serve this as a beverage or a dessert.

1 qt. vanilla ice cream,
    slightly softened

1/2 cup Tía María coffee liqueur
1/4 cup chocolate syrup
shaved chocolate

In covered blender container at medium speed, blend the ice cream, the coffee liqueur and the chocolate syrup JUST until smooth. Do not overblend; mixture should be thick. Serve immediately in 4 chilled glasses. Top with shaved chocolate.

Cook's Notes

Roadrunner, New Mexico state bird

¡Buena Suerte!
Good Luck!